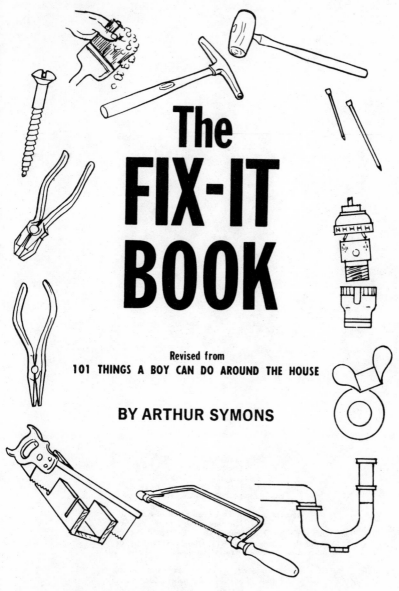

The
FIX-IT
BOOK

Revised from
101 THINGS A BOY CAN DO AROUND THE HOUSE

BY ARTHUR SYMONS

GRAMERCY PUBLISHING COMPANY • NEW YORK

This edition published by Gramercy Publishing Company,
a division of Crown Publishers, Inc.,
by arrangement with Sterling Publishing Co., Inc.

h

Contents

INTRODUCTION.. 5

PAINTING 7

Choosing Paint . . . Preparing the Surface for Painting . . .
Stirring the Paint . . . Applying the Paint . . . Closing a Paint
Can . . . Keeping Paintbrushes Clean . . . Making Emergency
Paintbrushes . . . Painting an Outside Metal Railing . . . Painting
Porch Steps . . . Painting in the Basement . . . Painting Concrete
Floors . . . Making Designs with Masking Tape . . . Tricks with
Luminous Paint . . . Painting Interior Walls and the Ceiling

KNOWING TOOLS 19

Learning to Buy Hand Tools . . . Knowing Your Screw Drivers
. . . Knowing Your Wood Screws . . . What to Do About a
Ruined Screw Head . . . Knowing Your Nuts and Bolts . . .
Knowing Your Measuring Tools . . . Knowing Your Wrenches
. . . Knowing Your Pliers . . . Knowing Your Hammers . . .
Knowing Your Saws . . . Knowing the Plane . . . Learning Nail
Language . . . The Right Way to Drive a Nail . . . Knowing
Lumber . . . Using Tools Instead of Muscle Power

EASY CREATIVE PROJECTS 40

Making Christmas Candlesticks . . . Making a Reel for Storing
Lines . . . Making Modern Plaques . . . Making Plaques for the
Den . . . Making a Loose-Leaf Binder . . . Making Bookshelves
. . . Making a Carrier for Firewood . . . Flooring an Attic . . .
Making a Table Lamp . . . Putting Wheels on Cabinets . . .
Making a Bird Feeder . . . Another Way to Mount the Bird
Feeder . . . Hanging a Pegboard . . . Making a Wastebasket

TAKING CARE OF THE FAMILY CAR............................. 56

Keeping a Maintenance Record . . . Keeping Tire Pressure at
the Right Level . . . Checking the Oil, Lights and Battery . . .
"Operation Tighten-Up" . . . Washing the Car . . . Marking
Your Lug Wrench . . . Changing a Tire . . . Making a Guide for
Putting the Car in the Garage . . . Getting Rid of Grease Spots
on the Garage Floor or Driveway

TAKING CARE OF THE LAWN, GARDEN AND HOUSE
PLANTS 67

Watering the Lawn . . . Giving a Plant a Long Drink . . . Cutting the Grass with a Rotary Mower . . . Edging the Lawn . . . Taking Care of Garden Tools . . . Hanging Garden Tools . . . Sorting Out Garden Sprays and Sprayers

TRICKS FOR EASIER HOME MAINTENANCE................... 75

Keeping a Notebook of Instructions for Appliances . . . Making a Schedule for Care of the Furnace . . . Taking Care of Electric Fans . . . Adjusting the Doors of Built-In Cabinets . . . Unsticking a Door . . . Repairing Warped Steps . . . Unsticking Windows . . . Caulking . . . Checking the Window Screens . . . Fixing Screen Doors that Sag . . . Preserving Screen Doors . . . Making Screens for Windows . . . Screening a Porch . . . Taking Care of Gutters and Leaders . . . Preventing Liquids from Freezing in the Winter . . . Mounting Things in Plaster

TAKING CARE OF THE PLUMBING AND HEATING...... 93

Finding the Main Shut-Off Valve, or "Operation Red Handle" . . . Unplugging Drains . . . More on Unplugging Drains: Using the "Snake" . . . Thawing Frozen Pipes . . . Fixing Toilet Tanks that Drip . . . Fixing Leaky Faucets . . . Fixing Clogged Garbage Disposals . . . What to Do About Gas Leaks . . . Saving Fuel . . . Fixing Leaky and Noisy Radiators

HOUSEHOLD ELECTRICITY 104

Finding the Main Switch . . . Learning Some Basic Electrical Terms . . . Basic Electrical Theory . . . Conductors, Insulators and Wiring . . . Checking the Fuses . . . Checking Electrical Wires . . . Removing a Broken Light Bulb . . . Replacing Broken Plugs the Easy Way . . . Installing a Cord Switch . . . Splicing Lamp Cord . . . Rewiring a Lamp . . . Taking Care of Various Electrical Appliances . . . Taking Care of a Television Set . . . Making a Crazy Light Box . . . Taking Care of a Radio

SAFETY IN THE HOME...124

Storing Inflammable Liquids . . . Preventing Spontaneous Combustion . . . Preventing Fires Caused by Furnaces and Stoves . . . Checking Ladders . . . Checking Railings . . . Keeping the Wind from Slamming Doors

INDEX...128

Introduction

Begin by doing the easy things and only go on to more difficult projects when you have mastered the simple ones. Don't move in on a potentially dangerous or costly project without thinking things through. Even more important, follow the safety rules to the letter. If you find you like these do-it-yourself projects and that you learn by experience, you have it made.

No book this size can offer more than a sketchy introduction to all the skills of the home handy man. If you do every project in the book you will merely have surveyed part of the field. The best home handy men I know are always learning, always trying new things, and often failing the first or second time they try something. Even keeping up with new materials and new tools as they are introduced on the market keeps you alert. It is an eye opener, for instance, to observe the new pegboard fixtures that appear at hardware stores every few months. The difference between the good home handy man and the bungler is a combination of willingness to try, imagination and ingenuity, forethought as to safety, and a refusal to consider a failure as anything but a contribution to the learning process.

One more thing—many a potential home handy man has been stopped in his tracks because he just wouldn't clean up after himself. Make sure you don't fall into this category.

Good luck!

Painting

I am starting this book with a chapter on painting because it *looks* like the easiest of the home handy man's chores. Actually, painting takes more know-how than many other home tasks, but even the most inexperienced person can get passable results by simply following the directions on the paint cans.

Your paint dealer, if he knows his stuff, can save you much grief if you talk with him about what you're going to do before you buy anything.

And don't forget to clean up after you have painted! It's much easier if you do it right away, before the paint hardens on the brushes and on the spattered spots.

The trick in painting is to get each coat on evenly and not too thick. Brush the paint into the surface, don't just smear it over the surface, and smooth out your strokes. Remember that two thin coats will look better and last longer than one thick coat.

Always read the directions on the can and follow them.

Choosing Paint. Get into the habit of reading the label on the paint can before you buy it or before you use it if you are using leftovers around the house.

There are so many kinds of paint that even the owners of paint stores have difficulty in keeping up with them. In many cases it isn't important which type you use but in other cases, the wrong kind of paint can get you into trouble. Paint meant for the interior of the house doesn't work so well outside. Enamel is hard and glossy, but it doesn't cover surfaces as well as flat paint. Some paints work fine on wood but will not hold on metal. There are special paints for concrete floors and for galvanized iron, and special paints to use in places where the weather is very moist.

Paints that come in pressure-type cans appear easy to use, but they actually take more skill to apply properly than the kinds that are applied with brushes and rollers. And what's worse, these pressurized paints cost much more per square foot of area covered than ordinary paints.

There are many new so-called synthetic-base paints that dry fast and have little odor. They work fine on interior walls and are good for some other uses but not for furniture or toys.

Preparing the Surface for Painting. More paint jobs have been ruined by slapping paint onto dirty, rough surfaces than in any other way. Be sure the surface to be painted is clean, smooth and dry. Wash it and clean it with a volatile fluid like turpentine or paint thinner. Be sure to remove all dust, dirt and grease.

If you have any ideas that paint will even out rough spots, you will learn differently. There must be no rough spots to begin with. You can fill in the cracks in plaster with any of the many types of plaster crack-filler on the market. On wood, if a scratch or gouge is too deep to remove with sandpaper, fill it with plastic wood, a special substance designed for this purpose; it comes in either paste or powder form. There is not much you can do about abused surfaces on metal.

If an object to be used outdoors has exposed steel screws or nail heads, daub some varnish or shellac over the steel. This will prevent rust streaks later.

If you are painting on new wood, first put shellac on knots and "bleeding" spots. Then use a coat of white paint, thinned with the proper thinner, before you paint for color.

Stirring the Paint. Opening and stirring a new can of paint separates the men from the boys, or the workmen from the daubers. There is a technique.

If the paint store has one of those oscillating mixers, fine. That's a start, but only a start.

Open the can carefully. I advise you not to use screw drivers for anything but driving screws; the exception to the rule is opening paint cans. There seems to be no better tool. Don't do all the opening from one side or you'll bend the lid. Pry a little bit about every 15 degrees around the circumference of the lid, so that the lid lifts easily all around.

Pour off about a third of the liquid into a clean container; a vegetable can with the lid cut all the way off will do. Now, with a small thin stick (the kind the paint dealer gives you is perfect except for the smallest cans), stir long and carefully until you are sure that there are no lumps and that all the paint in the can is of the same consistency. Pour back some of the light liquid you drained off at first. Stir. Pour back some more. Stir. By the time you have poured it all back, the paint should be uniform in thickness, with no lumps.

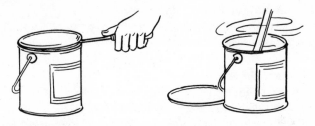

If you are using a can that has already been opened, with some of the paint gone, the problem is a bit different. Open the can carefully, as before. Inspect the paint. If there is a film on top of the paint, remove it carefully; be sure you get it all. Look at the consistency of the paint; if it is too thick, add just a bit of the thinner recommended on the label. It's easy to get too much thinner into the can, and then it's too late—the paint is ruined.

Then stir as if you were getting paid for it. When you think you have stirred enough, stir some more. Inspect the paint carefully with your stirring stick for lumps. You don't want any. When you have the paint the way you think it should be, try some—but on a piece of scrap wood, not on the object you intend to paint. If something is wrong, you will find out before you ruin the object of your painting intentions.

Applying the Paint. Try to do your painting in a place where there won't be any dust. Few things are as discouraging as an otherwise good paint job ruined by dust blowing in on it.

Once your paint is stirred and your surface prepared, what then?

Dip your brush into the paint. Don't, *please* don't, dip it in too far. Never dip it past one-third the length of the bristles. With practice you will learn just how deep to dip to suit your particular brushing technique. Wipe off some of the excess on the brush *lightly* against the inside of the rim. This is to assure that there isn't so much paint on the brush that it will drip, but that there is enough to make the stroke worth while.

Now paint. Brush the paint into the wood, following the grain. On metal choose your direction by the shape of the object. If you run into spots where the paint won't cover, try brushing these spots at a 90-degree angle, but finish with strokes in the proper direction. Jab the end of the brush into corners and other spots that are hard to reach, but always finish up with smooth, long strokes.

Get the coat of paint on evenly. Don't try to get it too thick. If there are thick spots, brush them out to a uniform thickness. If the paint begins to run, quickly smooth out the drip-lines with an almost dry brush before they begin to dry.

Have a rag handy to clean up spatters. If the job calls for it, use dropcloths to protect floors. Old shower curtains make fine dropcloths. Take time out occasionally to clean the paint from your hands if necessary. Paint-slippery hands don't give you the best control of your brush.

The rest is practice and experience.

Closing a Paint Can. When you have finished painting, you know you have to close the can to prevent the paint from drying out. Few people do it properly and carefully.

You think *you* know how to close a paint can ? Perhaps you do, but any person who has studied the theory of probability would make money by betting that most beginners don't know.

First, clean out the ridge in the top of the can—the ridge the lid fits into. Paper towels or rags will do for this job. If this ridge is particularly full of paint, you can salvage quite a bit of it with your brush.

Now get a rubber band that will fit around the can, and put it on at the level of the paint. Then you or anybody else in the house can tell without opening the can how much paint is in it.

Clean the lid so there are no paint blobs clinging to it that will prevent a good seal. Press the lid on carefully to be sure it is sealed properly all around. Then tap the lid a few light blows with a mallet. This extra minute of care might save you the paint that is left in the can. Few things are more discouraging than to open a can of paint you have been counting on to finish a job, only to find that careless closing has left nothing but a lump of colored goo.

Keeping Paintbrushes Clean. Most people love to paint and hate to clean their paintbrush, which often ends up in a pile of icky paintbrushes in odd corners of the basement or garage. Good paintbrushes are expensive; you can raise your handy-man status considerably by gathering and reconditioning all the paintbrushes around the house.

The time to clean a brush is *before* the paint gets hard. The easiest way is to buy a vapor-action brush conditioner from a mail-order house or paint store and follow the directions. This involves drilling small holes through the brush handles so they fit on the rack that holds them in the tightly sealed can. If you use enough fluid and aren't too impatient, the brushes will soften and the paint on the handles will strip away also. Then you can wash out the paint, first with turpentine, then with warm water and soap.

There are other brush cleaners on the market also. With all of them just follow the accompanying directions.

When the brushes are clean, wrap them carefully with wax paper and then newspaper, and hang them from the handle. Be sure they hang freely without leaning on anything; otherwise they will become bent.

If you take good care of the paintbrushes you use, you should have the privilege of informing all other members of the household that when they finish using a brush, they are to rinse it thoroughly and carefully with turpentine before it dries, then wash it with soap and warm water, and finally rewrap it and store it carefully.

MAKING EMERGENCY PAINTBRUSHES

For retouching jobs, for small jobs where you don't want to dirty a paintbrush, or for small precision work, the best tool is often a homemade brush. There are two principal types.

To make the first kind, cut off about 3 inches of manila rope. Bind one end with tape for a handle, and pull apart the strands at the other end. This is an excellent tool for retouching or small jobs.

The second kind of brush is for precision work, like retouching a scratch on the family car. It is made with a toothpick, a lollipop stick, or even a small piece of doweling. Dip a small part of one end into colorless nail polish or colorless airplane dope, and while it is still wet, twirl some cotton around the end to make the size "brush" you want. You can also use a cotton-tipped applicator, sold in drugstores, for the same purpose.

To get paint into a crack or otherwise inaccessible place, try getting a string wet with paint and run it through the crack.

PAINTING AN OUTSIDE METAL RAILING

Whether the metal railings outside your home are made of homely but useful pipe, or the finest ornamental iron, they deserve care. Without proper care they become unsightly or even dangerous. Rust is an enemy that doesn't give up easily and that often works under cover.

The real trick in painting outside metal-work is in proper preparation. The paintbrush is the *last* thing you reach for.

First, clean the metal thoroughly, with a wire brush, sandpaper, a file, or all three. Be sure that you remove all the loose paint and scale from the metal, and that there is no rust left. It is most important to remove the rust; don't leave it to become a source of ruin under your new paint.

After you are sure the rust, old paint and scale are all gone, go over the metal once more, this time with one of the petroleum grease-cutting products, like paint thinner. Let it dry.

Then paint the metal with a coat of metal preservative—red lead, or one of the commercial formulas that provide a rust-inhibiting base

under the paint. In an emergency an aluminum paint of good quality is better than nothing as a rust preventive, but I don't recommend it. Paint carefully, getting into the places that are hard to reach first and going over the surfaces that are easy to reach last. Brush out paint lumps and search carefully for "holidays," or uncovered areas. It's not how thick you spread the paint that counts, but how carefully you cover the whole surface.

After the preservative coat dries, do your final painting with a good grade of outdoor metal paint. Two thin coats are better than one thick one.

Don't paint outdoors if the temperature is lower than 50 degrees or higher than 90 degrees. If the temperature is too low, the paint won't dry properly, and if it is too high, the paint will dry so quickly that you can't smooth it out.

PAINTING PORCH STEPS

Wooden porch steps get more wear and bear the brunt of the weather more than any other part of the house. In most homes it is necessary to paint them every year if they are to last and be safe.

Don't just slap paint on them. It's a waste of paint and effort. Proper preparation is most important here.

Examine the wood carefully. If the finish is bad only in spots, scrape the bad spots with a putty knife; then use a wire brush and sandpaper, until you are *certain* that all the loose paint is gone. Smooth out scars; it is essential that the surface be smooth and not a water-trap.

Follow the scraping with a very thorough cleaning with benzine or paint thinner to get rid of grease and grime.

Cover the bare spots with an undercoat, preferably a special undercoat for outdoor floor surfaces. If there are only a few bare spots, cover them with your regular porch paint, thinned a bit. Don't put on the next coat until the undercoat is thoroughly dry.

Paint the boards the long way, making sure that you leave no "pinholes" and that you flow paint into the joints so that there will be no unpainted areas for air and water to attack. Brush the paint in well. Be careful the paint doesn't go on too thick; two thin coats will protect, whereas one thick coat will blister and break loose.

PAINTING IN THE BASEMENT

Some things you do around the house give you greater returns for the effort expended than others. One of the easiest ways to get a lot for your work is to paint the pipes and the posts in the basement with aluminum paint.

First, a word of caution—there are many grades of aluminum paint; for this purpose it pays to buy the best. The best goes farther and leaves a finish that looks almost like chrome. Buy a good quality aluminum paint that works equally well on wood and metal; it's available.

Start with the pipes—gas, hot water, and cold water. Clean them thoroughly with a soapy rag to remove grease, and then with a damp rag to remove the soap. Put dropcloths or newspapers under the place where you are working to catch the drip. Don't be an optimist; there will be drippings. If you find rust on the pipes, be sure to clean it off.

Use a brush with bristles no wider than 1 inch. Aluminum paint is very thin, so use just a bit on your brush. Get even coverage, and be sure you get full coverage. Otherwise you may have to go back looking for "holidays."

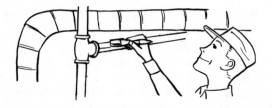

Be particularly careful not to let the paint get too thick around valve handles and faucets; if it's too thick it doesn't dry properly and everyone in the family will have aluminum-painted palms and fingers as souvenirs. Don't paint the gas meter; the gas company won't like it if you do.

When the pipes are finished, go to work on the metal posts and beams, remembering to clean them first of grease and rust, and to use dropcloths. By this time the basement will look brighter and cleaner as a whole, so that other things will show by their dinginess that they, too, could profit by a little dressing up. If you have doubts about painting any particular object, talk it over with the people who pay the bills.

PAINTING CONCRETE FLOORS

No matter how clean you keep a concrete floor, the top itself continues to turn into dust and it never looks quite clean. Paint is the answer, but since it is an expensive answer, think it over first.

Before you touch the paint, swab the floor thoroughly with detergent and water. If there are spots where oil has dropped, use a grease solvent, which you can get at a service station. Then, since concrete is loaded with alkali, any substance which is chemically the opposite of an acid, you may have to "cure" it with muriatic acid or one of the commercial preparations. Talk this one over with your paint dealer or your druggist. Floors more than four years old probably will not need curing.

After proper preparation of the floor, the type of paint you use will make or break the job. There are several different types of paint on the market designed for concrete floors, some with a rubber base, some with synthetic bases. Ask your paint dealer for advice.

Then paint. It might take two coats, depending on the covering power. Brush evenly, don't overload the brush, and don't use a brush so large that it will tire you too soon. Painters can drag a 6-inch brush through paint all day long and never feel it, but you might find you can get more work done, with less fatigue, using a 3- or 4-inch brush or a roller.

Be careful around the walls; remember that you're only supposed to be painting the floor. Use a smaller brush in the corners; you will have better control.

Now for garages, here is the crowning touch. There are spots where water brought in by the car creates a slippery surface, and this can be dangerous. The "fix" is easy and it's fun.

After the painted floor has dried, mark off these dangerous areas with chalk. Put another coat of paint on these spots, and while the paint is still wet, scatter dry sand over it with your hands, with a laundry sprinkler, or with a can with holes punched in its bottom. Don't use too much sand; use your judgment about the least amount that will provide the best non-slip surface. Of course the sand won't stick to the dry paint, so don't worry about the sand that falls off the newly painted areas. When the non-slip part dries, you can sweep the excess sand off the other part of the floor without a bit of trouble.

MAKING DESIGNS WITH MASKING TAPE

Have you ever wondered how people no more talented than you are able to paint geometric designs on water skis, bobsleds, and other possessions? Maybe they do it with masking tape.

Masking tape comes in various widths, and you can cut it down to the width you want if it is too wide.

Let's say the project is a pair of water skis, and you want white diamonds on red skis. You will have to do it backwards. Paint the skis white. When the paint dries, make your design with masking tape, and repaint the exposed area of the skis red. When you remove the masking tape, there is the design.

TRICKS WITH LUMINOUS PAINT

A $\frac{1}{2}$-ounce jar of luminous paint will cost about 50 cents; for many households this can be a very wise investment. Here are some of the things you can do with it (you can dream up more for your own home):

Outline a keyhole that can't be found easily in the dark.

Put a spot of it on the pull of an old-fashioned light that goes on by pulling a cord.

Put a couple of spots on the edge of the door that people walk into at night.

Put a spot on the end of a flashlight to make it easy to find in the dark.

Put a spot on the plate surrounding a light switch to make it easier to find.

If your house is in an area where there are frequent power failures, put a spot of luminous paint on your oil lamp, lanterns, or box of candles.

PAINTING INTERIOR WALLS AND THE CEILING

When you are ready to paint an interior wall, you have arrived. This is one time when, with patience and care, you can do a job that will really cinch your reputation as a "do-it-yourselfer." Besides it's fun.

Move all the furniture out if possible. If not, cover it with dropcloths or newspapers to protect it. Protect the floors the same way, too.

Brush down the ceiling and walls to get rid of dust, loose paint, and loose plaster.

When the walls are as clean as you can get them by brushing, look for cracks to be patched. Hairline cracks can be covered with a special pencil that looks like a big fat crayon. Cracks too thick for this treatment can be filled with a chalk powder immersed in oil which is called spackling compound (spackling paste is even better); follow the directions on the can. Large holes and cracks will require patching plaster; again, read the directions on the package and remember, before you paint, to use a primer over the places where you used patching plaster. Don't try to paint over a small crack; it will show through.

Drop the shell of the lighting fixture if there is one in the ceiling; there's no need to remove the entire fixture. When the shell is replaced it will cover very well the uneven line around the light.

When you paint the ceiling, use very little paint on your brush; that will prevent much of the drip to your wrist. Don't worry about painting an inch or two down the walls with the ceiling paint; you'll be covering it anyhow. Don't try to do the ceiling from anything but a good, solid folding ladder, or a *strong* board (at least 2 inches thick) between two ladders. Stand so that your head is about 6 inches from the ceiling. Keep the windows nearly closed to avoid dust and uneven drying.

Start in a corner and try to keep the light at your back; you can see better that way. Paint along the short dimension of the room; you will blend your strokes better.

When you start the walls, begin in a corner and paint down from the top. If you are right-handed, start with the right-hand wall of the corner so you can brace yourself with your left hand on the dry portion of the wall.

Do a strip from 2 to 4 feet wide and make it wider at the top than at the bottom. When you start the next strip, if the blended places are not perfectly vertical lines they won't be so noticeable. Have a small brush handy for the tricky part of separating the wall color from the ceiling color, and for getting into the corners.

Use the small brush around doorways, windows, and so forth; it's easier to control.

Painting with a roller instead of a brush is more popular than ever now. It is especially useful for painting ceilings.

For a really super job, ask your paint dealer if a roller stippler will work with the type of paint you are using; all you do with a roller stippler is run it along the newly painted wall while it is still wet. It gives you a smoother, more uniform finish. This step is unnecessary if you paint with a roller instead of a brush.

Knowing Tools

When aviation cadets report for training, they are often unhappy because they spend months in classrooms before they ever get an opportunity to fly an airplane. This section is much like a "ground school." It will tell you about the tools you need and how to use them to carry out many of the later projects in the book.

Become familiar with the information here, then come back to it as you need it.

Almost anybody can do a "butcher's job" with the wrong tool, or a tool that isn't used properly, or one that hasn't been properly cared for. For this you don't need a book; all you need are plenty of bandages, a spare finger or two, and complete indifference to what the job looks like when it's finished.

The best work requires patience, good measuring, tools that are well cared for, and a bit of experience. You can always do a better job the second time around. Don't worry, though, about mistakes; if you never do anything you'll avoid mistakes, but doing nothing isn't much fun.

Next most important to having the proper tools is being able to find them, and then finding them in good condition. Have a place for each tool, and keep it in that place. Keep the tools clean also. Dirty, greasy tools don't do a job properly, and their very greasiness breeds accidents because they slip in your hand. Keep cutting tools sharp.

In my own library I have several large books that cover the uses of tools, so this short chapter is obviously one that can hit only a few of the high spots.

LEARNING TO BUY HAND TOOLS

Trying to do good work with the wrong tools or tools of poor quality is a losing proposition. There are a few simple rules for buying tools, and following them can save you many disappointments.

First, a few tools of high quality are better than a whole basement filled with junk. You will be surprised at how few tools you can get by with if you have to. Don't ever compromise by buying three tools of low quality when the same amount of money would buy two good ones.

Second, buy "name brands," or do your shopping at retail outlets of nationally known mail-order houses. Even big stores usually have two qualities of tools—buy the better quality. Be cautious when buying in "surplus sales" stores. You can often pick up something good, but you have to know your tools before you buy.
pick up something good, but you have to know your tools before you buy.

One of the big mistakes of many people who go shopping for tools is buying unlikely combinations. Think twice before you buy sets or combination tools that are touted to do all sorts of things. Especially poor buys are combinations of tools that fit into one handle. They just won't do the job you expect.

Now about price. If you deal with your local hardware merchant and get to know him, you will find that his prices are fair and that he can help you considerably with your selections. The big bargain or chain hardware stores are often less helpful. The big national mail-order companies may be a few cents over on some items or a few cents under on others, but on the average their prices are fair and competitive.

Don't buy a tool just because you have the money and you feel you might be able to use the tool some day. Buy tools as you need them. I have been doing my own puttering around for thirty years and have never found a use for my wrecking bar. When I bought it, it seemed so necessary.

Buy tools that fit you *now*. If you're the chess type instead of the football type, don't buy a heavy hammer that you can't control with your weak wrist muscles; buy a lighter one that will respond to your guidance. You can buy the heavy one later, and the light one will be useful for driving small brads and for light tapping.

Always remember to clean each tool after use, put it where it belongs, and oil it lightly against rust if you're not going to use it for a while.

KNOWING YOUR SCREW DRIVERS

The most abused tools in most houses are screw drivers. People use them carelessly for chisels, crowbars, hammers, can openers and scrapers, or they use screw drivers with blades that are too small or too large for the screw heads. Then they wonder why they tear up screw heads and get the blades through their hands.

The blade of a screw driver should be square and straight. The part of the blade that fits into the screw slot should *not* have any taper. The blade should not protrude beyond the outside of the screw head, and it should fit snugly from side to side. If the blade is wider than the screw slot, the blade will tear up the slot; the blade should fit snugly. Look at this:

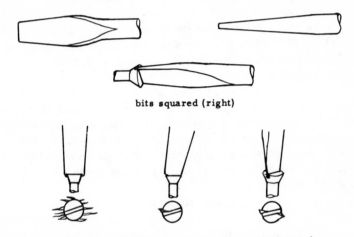

bits squared (right)

bits rounded or incorrect size for screw (wrong)

For safety's sake, don't hold the work in one hand while you use the screw driver with the other. More people get holes in their hands that way. Hold the work in a vise if necessary.

If you have to get extra pressure on a screw driver, put your other hand on top of the tool while you turn. Don't use pliers or a wrench for turning a screw. And don't pound the head of a screw driver with a hammer or other tool.

You just can't have too many sizes of screw drivers around the house.

Look at the illustration:

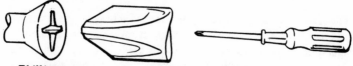

Phillips screw   Phillips screwdriver bit

This will tell you most of what you need to know about Phillips screws, a special kind of screw with a cross-shaped slot. Use a Phillips screw driver, not an ordinary screw driver, on a Phillips screw. The ordinary screw driver might work, but the chances are the screw head will never be the same again.

KNOWING YOUR WOOD SCREWS

For some reason that is hidden from mere mortals, you will discover that, among the hundreds of wood screws around the house, you rarely find exactly the one you need. This means going to the hardware store; you might as well learn to talk screw language before you go.

Wood screws are divided into two main classes: steel, and brass or aluminum. Steel screws come in different finishes, such as bright (just plain steel), blued, or japanned (enameled). Brass screws cost more, but they are more satisfactory for jobs where appearance counts, and for use outside, where rain and humidity might cause steel screws to rust. You wouldn't want to use a steel screw in building a boat, nor would you want large brass screws for a workbench.

There are three types of screw heads:

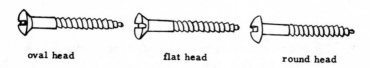

oval head   flat head   round head

Flat heads are cheaper, easier to work with, and easier to conceal. When you want a smooth surface, you can easily get a screw with a flat head to go below the surface.

Round heads and oval heads are fine for ornamental effects.

Once you decide on the metal, finish, and shape of head, then you must consider the size of the screw you want. This is a real dilemma if you don't know the nomenclature. Look at the table below:

Screw No.	Body Diameter	Diameter of Round head	Diameter of Flat head
0	0.060	0.106	0.112
1	.073	.130	.138
2	.086	.154	.164
3	.099	.178	.190
4	.112	.202	.216
5	.125	.226	.242
6	.138	.250	.268
7	.151	.275	.294
8	.164	.298	.320
9	.177	.322	.346
10	.190	.347	.372
11	.203	.370	.393
12	.216	.394	.424
14	.242	.442	.476
16	.268	.490	.528
18	.294	.539	.580
20	.320	.587	.632
24	.372	.683	.736

Tell the hardware dealer the length, screw number and type of head; tell him also whether you want brass or steel, and if you want steel, specify the kind of finish you want.

The diameter figures are in thousands of an inch. Oval heads have the same diameter as flat heads. Not all screw numbers come in all lengths. A 6-inch No. 2 would be nothing more than a piece of thin wire with grooves in it, and a ½-inch No. 20 would be almost as thick as long.

Try to choose screws of a length and number thick enough to hold your pieces of wood together, but not so thick that they will split the wood when going in.

I have successfully used ⅜-inch No. 7's to attach hinges to ½-inch plywood, because they are very heavy screws for their length.

One more thing. You are bound to have some screws left over. Try to keep them sorted as to length and thickness. If you keep them in order, you'll save time when you need a screw in a hurry.

WHAT TO DO ABOUT A RUINED SCREW HEAD

Even though they know better, people try to loosen or tighten screws with a screw driver of the wrong size. The result is that the slot is so worn that no screw driver can grip it properly.

There are two possible ways to repair the damage long enough to get the screw out so it can be replaced with a new one.

By careful sawing with a hack-saw blade, you might be able to widen, straighten and square the slot so that a slightly larger screw driver will fit into it neatly and do the job; or by careful filing, you might be able to cut down the shoulders of the screw so that a small wrench will fit it.

KNOWING YOUR NUTS AND BOLTS

You will probably hardly ever buy bolts for new projects, but chances are, if you are the home handy man, you will buy them to replace those worn out in service or lost by the younger children. Look at the illustration:

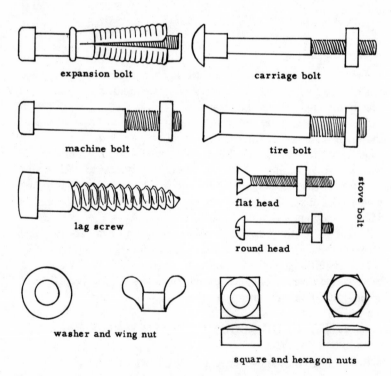

expansion bolt

carriage bolt

machine bolt

tire bolt

lag screw

flat head

round head

stove bolt

washer and wing nut

square and hexagon nuts

When you buy them, the easy way is to take the old one with you, but that's a bit tough if it's lying under the maple tree down at the corner or if it got thrown out with the trash. That doesn't matter, though, if you ask for the proper type of bolt and specify length and diameter; for nuts and washers, specify shape and diameter. Study the chart.

KNOWING YOUR MEASURING TOOLS

Folding Rule. You can't do much around the house without one of these. Be sure that you can read the one you use and that you know what fraction of an inch the individual marks represent. The longest lines between the numbered inches show half-inches. The next longest show quarters of an inch. The next longest show eighths of an inch. The shortest lines on most rules show sixteenths of an inch. With a little practice you will be able to read these measurements without counting. Keep the rule clean, and keep the joints oiled very lightly.

Squares. There are two types: the carpenter's square and the try square. They look like this:

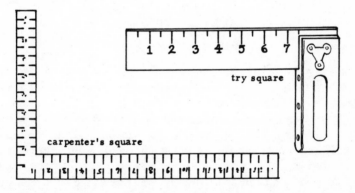

try square

carpenter's square

Never trust your eye for measuring a right angle; you'll be wrong. Use the square. Hold the handle and the blade snugly against the work when you draw your lines, and check more than once to be sure you are holding them snugly. If you are going to fasten two boards together, they had better be square or your work will look like a nursery-rhyme illustration. Use the try square to check your work.

Pencil. Yes, this is a measuring tool. Use a *sharp* No. 2½ for marking off points that you need to see on the work. The sharper the pencil, the thinner the line is. Harder pencils may mar your work and be difficult to see while softer ones will lose their point too fast.

Compass. You won't need this often; when you do, use a simple one such as used by schoolchildren. Just be certain the joint is tight and the pencil sharp.

KNOWING YOUR WRENCHES

There are many types of wrenches, most of them designed for specific purposes. In most homes, however, there are only one or two types, and the home mechanic has to make do with what he has. Before I go on to discussing wrenches for turning nuts, let's take a look at one particular type that is not used for this purpose.

The pipe wrench, or Stillson wrench, is used for turning pipes or other round objects. It looks like a monkey wrench, but it has springs and a jaw that wiggles a bit. The purpose of the loose jaw is to get a better grip on the pipe. It looks like this:

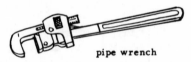

pipe wrench

When you turn the pipe clockwise, the open jaw points to the left; when you turn the pipe counterclockwise, the open jaw points to the right. Try it on a broom handle; if you work from the correct direction the loose jaw makes the wrench clamp tighter; try it the other way and the wrench slips. You don't have to take the wrench off the pipe after you have turned it; to make it grip the pipe tightly again, just push the wrench down.

Keep the jaws clean and sharp. If you are working with pipe you don't want to scar, cover it with adhesive tape to protect it from the wrench's jaws.

Most homes have an adjustable wrench, sometimes called a monkey wrench. It looks like this:

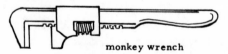

monkey wrench

These are useful for turning large nuts; their awkwardness creates no problems, but if the adjustable feature gets loose or if you don't adjust the wrench just right, you end up grinding the corners off the nuts. Adjustable end wrenches are handier to use, but they become loose-jawed also.

Box wrenches and open-end wrenches are the best kind, but you must be sure that when you use them they fit the nut you wish to turn. They look like this:

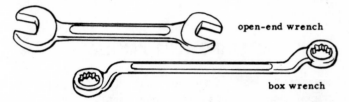

open-end wrench

box wrench

There are many other types of specialized wrenches, including socket wrenches; if your home has these other types, someone there undoubtedly knows how to use them.

KNOWING YOUR PLIERS

People use pliers for almost anything, often when they shouldn't. What is worse, they often use the wrong pliers for the right job. Below are the three main types of pliers:

slip-joint   long-nosed   side-cutting

The ones on the left are adjustable pliers (sometimes called slip-joint pliers). These are the ones to use for most jobs *except turning nuts*. Use a wrench to save the nut, your fingers and your patience.

The ones in the center are long-nosed pliers. These are rather delicate. They can act as extensions of your fingers in tight spots and can twist light wire. They also have a place in your box of fishing tackle.

Don't use them for heavy work because you'll spring the jaws and ruin the pliers.

Side-cutting pliers, on the right, are used mostly in electrical work. They are strong enough to grip and twist heavy wire and to crush the insulation on wires by gripping and squeezing the insulation in the bottom of the jaws below the joint.

When cutting heavy wire, nick the wire and bend it. Then cut at the bent point with the slot part of the pliers. You can cut wire also with the slip-joint pliers; you'll find the part with which to cut right above the joint.

KNOWING YOUR HAMMERS

There are many kinds of hammers (and I'll include mallets in this classification), and it's a good idea to know what they are for.

The old reliable claw hammer, or carpenter's hammer, is the basic tool for the home. You can drive nails or pull them with it. You can use it to knock things apart or to tap a board into place.

Just remember a few things about these hammers. It's the speed of the hammer blows, not the strength behind each blow, that does the work. The hammer works best when you grip it at the end of the handle rather than part way up, but if you are not as strong as a carpenter, grip it where it feels best for your strength and swing. When drawing nails out with a claw hammer, remember that the further you pull the nail head out of the wood the more leverage you lose. As soon as you begin to lose leverage, slip a block under the hammer claws and your leverage will be as good as new.

Be sure your hammer is in good shape. See that the hammer head is fastened securely to the handle. A flying hammer head can do a lot of damage.

If the face (the part that hits the nail) is chipped or scarred, other pieces might chip off and fly or the head may slip off the work.

Keep the handle and the head free from grease and loose dirt. Greasy hammer handles and heads slip and can hurt somebody.

Don't use a metal-headed hammer to drive a chisel or to jam one board against another. You can ruin more chisel handles and boards this way. This is the place to use the mallet, which, if you don't know, looks

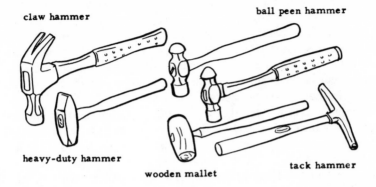

claw hammer

ball peen hammer

heavy-duty hammer

wooden mallet

tack hammer

like an overgrown gavel. A rubber mallet is often useful to have around the house. It is especially useful for bumping out dents in objects made of sheet metal.

Machinist's hammers, or ball-peen hammers, have limited uses around the house. I have never had occasion to use mine.

A heavy-duty hammer with a 3-pound head is very useful for driving stakes and for general heavy work where a sledge hammer isn't quite the ticket because of its large size and long handle.

KNOWING YOUR SAWS

Hand Saws. These are the old reliable saws that you see carpenters using. They look like this:

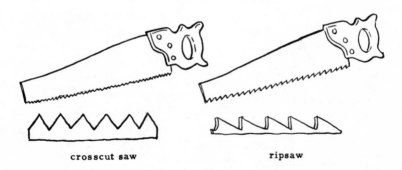

crosscut saw

ripsaw

Hand saws come in two main classifications: ripsaws and crosscut saws. You can tell the difference between these two types by the teeth. Ripsaws cut with the grain, or along the length of the board, while crosscut saws are designed to cut across the grain. For a diagonal cut use the crosscut unless the cut is almost parallel to the grain of the wood. Hold the crosscut saw at about a 45-degree angle, and the ripsaw at about a 60-degree angle. They work better that way.

The more teeth to the inch, the smoother is the cut. Also, the more teeth to the inch, the more work it is to cut the same amount of wood. When you hear the hardware man talk about "points" in a saw, he is not using doubletalk. There is always one less tooth to the inch than there are points. If 1 inch bridges the *points* of 6 teeth, there are 5 teeth to the inch. My own crosscut saw is an 8-point job, and it's a pretty good compromise.

Like most tools, and like all cutting tools, hand saws must be sharp to do a good job. Sharpening saws is a lot of work; they not only have to be sharpened, but they also have to be "set" properly. By "set," I mean that every other tooth is bent in alternate directions from the whole blade itself. The cut you make with the saw (called the *kerf*) will be as wide as the set. If the saw sticks in the kerf, it may be that the set needs looking after.

On the other hand, hard dragging on the saw could mean that it is rusty or needs sharpening or both. You can take care of the rust with oil and steel wool. I recommend that you have the job of sharpening or setting done by the local hardware store.

When you saw, do most of your cutting when you pull the blade toward you; use very little pressure when you push it away from you. Occasionally you may forget this, and a bent saw will remind you of the

rule. You can straighten slight kinks in a saw by using your hands. To straighten more serious bends, lay the saw flat on the workbench with the handle hanging over the bench, not on it. Beat on the saw carefully with a mallet, *not* a hammer. You can tell if it is straight by sighting along the straight edge of the blade.

Before you saw, draw a line on the board, and when you saw, do *not* saw the line away. Saw *beside* the line. This way you compensate for the width of the kerf and you will obtain a board of the dimension you want. Start any saw cut with a series of very light nicks, so you are sure the cut will start in the proper place before your saw bites in, and so you have a groove to hold the saw and keep it from jumping off the board and cutting your knuckles.

You can hold the board to the workbench in a vise, with C-clamps, or on a sawhorse with your knees. Just be sure that the board is held firmly and that the vise or clamps don't gouge the wood. Support the piece that is about to drop off, so when it falls it doesn't take with it a large splinter that will ruin the work.

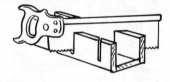

Backsaw. The backsaw is the one with the heavy metal back that is used with a miter box. It usually has more teeth to the inch than ordinary saws, so it is used occasionally for especially smooth cuts. Backsaws come in different sizes, but chances are the one at your house was meant to fit your miter box and you won't have much choice as to size. Since the backsaw is very rigid, you might use it for cuts very close to the end of a board.

Compass saw. This is sometimes called a keyhole saw. It is used to get into tight places a hand saw won't reach and for sawing slight curves. It looks like this:

31

Coping saw. This is essentially a hand-operated jig saw. You can cut all sorts of complicated curves with a coping saw. If you want to cut from the *inside* of a board, drill a hole in the board large enough for the blade of the saw to go through, remove the blade from the saw, pass the blade through the hole, leaving the handle outside, put the saw together again, and you're in business. It looks like this:

Hack saw. This saw is used for cutting metal. The blade is removable, and you use a new one rather than trying to get the old one sharpened. The blades don't last very long.

For cutting different metals, there are different blades with different numbers of points and different stiffnesses. A blade with about 17 points and a medium stiffness is a good compromise for all-round household work. It looks like this:

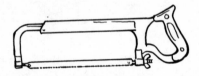

The teeth point *away* from the handle; you use pressure only on the stroke *away* from you. You may use both hands on the hack saw, one at each end of the saw. When you use the hack saw, hold it so the greatest possible number of teeth engage the work. Work on the flat of the metal, if possible. Hold the work firmly in a vise. And beware of breaking blades; they can give you a nasty cut.

KNOWING THE PLANE

Most home workshops include one or more planes, and most planes in most home workshops aren't in operating order. This is because adjusting, sharpening, and maintaining a plane take patience—a rare commodity at present.

There really is no reason to let a plane bluff you. It is nothing more than an assortment of parts, and most of the parts don't have to be monkeyed with. Below is a drawing of a plane, right out of the U.S. Army's manual on carpentry:

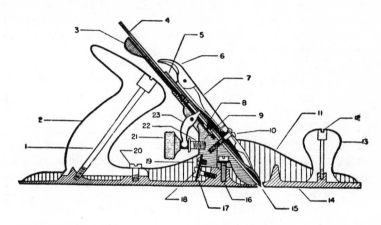

1. Handle bolt and nut.	13. Knob.
2. Handle.	14. Face.
3. Lateral adjusting lever.	15. Throat.
4. Blade.	16. Frog screw.
5. Cap-iron or blade.	17. Frog clip.
6. Cam lever.	18. Frog adjusting screw.
7. Cap.	19. Frog clip screw.
8. Cap-iron screw.	20. Handle toe bolt.
9. Frog.	21. Adjusting nut.
10. Cap screw.	22. Cutter adjusting screw.
11. Plane bottom.	23. Y-adjustment lever.
12. Knob bolt and nut.	

There are three main types of planes:

The *smoothing plane* is from $5\frac{1}{2}$ to 10 inches long, and the blade is perfectly straight across the bottom.

The *jack plane* is about $11\frac{1}{2}$ inches long, and the bottom of the blade is curved.

The *block plane* is about 4 inches long; it differs from the smoothing plane by having no cap iron and by the fact that the bevel of the blade points up instead of down.

The smoothing plane is the jack-of-all-trades, and you can get by with only this in the house. The jack plane is for hurry-up jobs, where deep and fast cutting is necessary; you clean up after it with the smoothing plane. The block plane is for cutting end grain.

Now, some of the tricks of the trade.

Adjusting the blade in the plane is often the difference between success and failure. Set the bottom of the cap about $\frac{1}{8}$ of an inch above the cutting edge of the blade for a jack plane, and about $\frac{1}{32}$ of an inch for a smoothing plane. Hold the plane upside down in your left hand, and look down along the face. Turn the adjusting nut until the blade is just a trifle above the face. Make the blade parallel with the face by moving the adjusting lever. For deeper cuts you can move the blade up more than a trifle, but if you move it too far you've had it. A little practice will show you just how far you can go.

Always plane with the grain of the wood instead of against it, as shown in the illustration; note that the grain runs in the direction which permits the blade to slice across it, rather than dig into it. Keep the plane at a slight angle to the direction of the stroke so it moves slightly crab-wise. For some reason it cuts better this way.

Don't drag any plane backward on the wood; this dulls the blade quickly. Lift it on the return stroke.

To sharpen a blade, use a well-oiled oilstone, and learn to hold the blade at the same angle as the present bevel of the blade. To remove the blade, pull the cam lever, remove the lever cap, and loosen the screw.

When you use the jack or smoothing plane, bear down on the front end of the plane at the beginning of the stroke and on the rear of the plane at the end of the stroke. It seems easier to do just the opposite, but then the result is a curved line instead of a straight one. See the illustration:

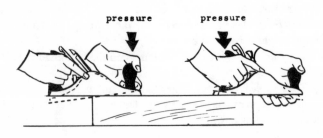

When you use the block plane, use it with one hand. Take short strokes, and don't let the plane run over the far end of the board. If you must plane near the edge, clamp or nail a block of wood at the edge to prevent chipping, like this:

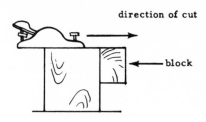

direction of cut

block

LEARNING NAIL LANGUAGE

There are more types and sizes of nails than there are ways of flunking algebra. The illustration will show you *some* of them:

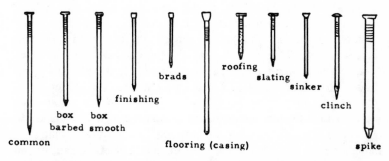

brads

roofing

slating

sinker

finishing

clinch

box
barbed

box
smooth

common

flooring (casing)

spike

Most of the time you will be using common nails, brads, and finishing nails. Finishing nails have small heads, which make them fairly inconspicuous and easy to cover for fine work. A brad, for all practical purposes, is a small finishing nail. Common nails are a bit thicker for their length than finishing nails and brads and are therefore easier to drive without bending.

The language used to describe the size of nails has been due for a change for many years, but nobody makes the move. Those who know what the size language means probably don't want to let anyone else in on the secret. They're like a gang with secret passwords, but the passwords aren't too hard to fathom. The "d" means penny, as in English money. Here is the table:

Size	Length (inches)	Approximate Number per Pound
2d	1	900
3d	$1\frac{1}{4}$	615
4d	$1\frac{1}{2}$	320
5d	$1\frac{3}{4}$	250
6d	2	200
7d	$2\frac{1}{4}$	150
8d	$2\frac{1}{2}$	100
9d	$2\frac{3}{4}$	85
10d	3	75

Nails run in size up to 60d spikes, but 10d is the largest you need for ordinary household do-it-yourselfing.

The trick is to choose the right nail for the job. You don't want one so big that it will go all the way through both boards, or so small that it won't hold. Oversize nails often split the wood. To nail two boards side to side, choose a nail that will go through the top board and about three quarters of the way through the bottom board. To nail two boards together, side grain to end grain, choose a nail that will go through the top board and about $1\frac{1}{4}$ to $1\frac{1}{2}$ times the thickness of the top board into the edge of the other. If this means using a nail that is so thick you are afraid it will split the wood, you can get around the problem in one of two ways. You can drill a hole where the nail will go, being sure, though, that the hole is less than half the diameter of the nail; or you can cut the point of the nail off, leaving a blunt end. This will cut the wood instead of separating and splitting it.

THE RIGHT WAY TO DRIVE A NAIL

The right way to drive a nail is easy to learn, but very few people know how to do it. By learning one little trick you can drive your nail straight almost every time.

When you start the nail, place the point where it should go, but *incline the head away from you about* 10 *degrees*. Like this:

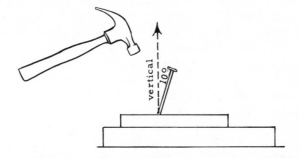

Start hammering with little taps until you are sure the friction of the board is holding the nail firmly. Then begin to whack it with long strokes, being sure that when the hammer head hits the nail head, it does so squarely and surely. The arc of the hammer swing will straighten that 10-degree "lean," and drive the nail straight down.

When you get the nail head close to the wood, be careful. If it is a very small nail, use a nail set to finish the job. A nail set is a tool for driving the head of the nail below the surface. If it is a large nail, a nail set won't help, but be sure you are hitting the nail head and not the wood.

KNOWING LUMBER

Lumber takes a lot of knowing, and an honest lumber dealer is your only guarantee that you won't go astray. Most lumber dealers, bless 'em, are honest men who try to give you the right lumber for the job. But they're busy men, too, so you must co-operate. Tell the man exactly what you have in mind (a rough drawing helps considerably), and see him, if possible, on a weekday instead of Saturday, when every do-it- yourselfer in the neighborhood is clamoring for his attention.

For some jobs the poorer grades of lumber are good enough, but for others you need the best. The difference in price is tremendous, so it pays not to get a better grade than the job requires. The same goes for the variety of wood. Local oak or sugar pine may cost less than half as much as Douglas fir or more exotic woods. Let your dealer help you decide.

You can also waste a lot of money by buying the wrong lengths of the right kind of lumber. If you need three 5-foot pieces, a 16-foot length makes much more sense than two 12's or three 8's. For larger projects, make up a bill of materials, which is nothing more than a list of the pieces you need by size. If you catch your dealer when he is not busy, he will be glad to help you make up the bill of materials.

Remember when you order lumber that a board 2 inches by 4 inches (thickness and width) isn't 2 inches by 4 inches; it's actually $1\frac{5}{8}$ inches by $3\frac{5}{8}$ inches. This piece started out measuring 2 inches by 4 inches, but when its surface was planed down to the smoothness you expect, it lost $\frac{3}{8}$ of an inch of its width and its thickness.

S4S lumber (surfaced four sides) runs to about the following dimensions:

Stated Size (inches)		Actual Size (inches)	
Thickness	*Width*	*Thickness*	*Width*
1	4	25/32	$3\frac{5}{8}$
1	6	25/32	$5\frac{5}{8}$
1	8	25/32	$7\frac{1}{2}$
1	10	25/32	$9\frac{1}{2}$
1	12	25/32	$11\frac{1}{2}$

When you order your lumber, ask for it by dimension and length, as in, "I want two 2-by-4's twelve feet long," or "I need a 1-by-12 eight feet long." (This usually appears as $2'' \times 4''$ or $1'' \times 12''$.)

Lumber is priced in board feet; a board foot is a cubic measurement. One board foot is 1 inch thick, 12 inches long, and 12 inches wide. The two $2'' \times 4''$ s twelve feet long would work out to 24 board feet— $\frac{1}{3}$ (the width, 4 inches, is $\frac{1}{3}$ of a foot) times 12 (the length in feet) times $\frac{1}{6}$ (the thickness, 2 inches, is $\frac{1}{6}$ of a foot) times 2 (the number of pieces).

Plywood and other wooden sheet products are sold by the square foot instead of by the board foot. Moldings and that type of specialty are sold by the running foot, or everyday linear foot.

Grades of lumber depend on the straightness of the pieces, the number of knots, splits or other defects, and other factors. You will just have to take your dealer's word for the grade because you can't learn to grade lumber from a book.

USING TOOLS INSTEAD OF MUSCLE POWER

The professional workman can work all day at a tough job partly because he knows how to do things the easy way. He knows how to use his muscles, but he also knows how to save them. Here are a few tricks of some of the trades. Once you get the idea you can do some thinking of your own along these lines.

Suppose you have to take a large door off its hinges, either to let a large piece of furniture through the door or to make a repair. If it is a heavy door and you don't have any help, it's like threading a needle with boxing gloves to slide the door portion of the hinges into the jamb portion just right and hold it there while you sink the pin that holds the hinges in place. It would be so much easier if you were to cut a stick to just the right thickness, place it on the floor, and slide the door into the right spot, using the stick to hold it up just the right amount.

The same idea will help you change a tire. Modern tires and wheels are heavy, and holding the wheel with one hand while you try to line up the lug bolts isn't the world's easiest maneuver. Use a $2'' \times 4''$ board to hold the weight. Jack the car up or down as necessary to make the 2-inch dimension just right, and slide the wheel along the board right into the lug bolts.

An old-fashioned automobile jack (not the bumper type) can do many odd jobs, like lifting a flight of outdoor wooden steps while you slide bricks under them to level the steps, or bending a piece of heavy pipe. A bumper jack can be useful in lifting a fence post out of the ground if you don't want to go to the trouble of digging it out.

Don't try to tighten a wire fence by pulling on it by hand; you can get further faster by using turnbuckles and wire.

Often a few minutes spent building a ramp rather than lifting a heavy object several inches is well spent.

This idea breaks down, however, when you try to apply it to getting more leverage on tools. If the wrench won't turn the nut, don't add an extension to the wrench handle—you will break the wrench or tear up the nut or both. Better try some "liquid wrench" to loosen the rust rather than "Jack Armstrong" methods.

Easy Creative Projects

If you haven't used your hands much to make things, it's best to start out making easy things. Wood is always fun to work with, and small projects in wood don't cost much because you can often get wood scraps for nothing.

Here are a few projects that you can play around with, with a very good possibility of getting worth-while results.

Don't give up a project if you're unsuccessful with it the first time Just try again, and learn from your mistakes.

MAKING CHRISTMAS CANDLESTICKS

One of my wife's most treasured possessions is a pair of Christmas candlesticks our son made for her as a Cub Scout project. It is a very simple project and one that brings great satisfaction in return for a small investment in time.

The candlesticks are made from a log about 10 inches long and about 5 inches in diameter. Remember, I said "about," since there is nothing sacred about these dimensions. You can make it larger or smaller depending on what sort of log you can find and where the candlesticks are to be used.

Choose a log that has good, tight, interesting bark.

Taking care not to injure the bark, cut the log lengthwise down the center, like this:

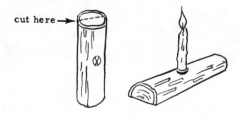

cut here →

If you put it in a vise, wrap a towel around the log. Plane the surfaces opened up by the saw, and make everything except the bark just as smooth as you can. Use sandpaper, scrapers, or any other tools or equipment that will smooth wood.

Measure the diameter of a pair of Christmas candles. Drill a hole of the proper diameter and about $\frac{3}{4}$ of an inch deep in each half of the log.

Varnish the entire log carefully, sanding the wood lightly but not the bark after each application of varnish.

Dress it with evergreen boughs or Christmas ribbon, and you have a pair of candlesticks that will make a very attractive mantel or table decoration.

MAKING A REEL FOR STORING LINES

Ropes used for towing in water skiing, anchor lines for small boats, clotheslines, and other kinds of rope and line get into tangles at the least provocation. You can make a very simple reel that will keep these lines untangled and ready for use, and you can do it with simple tools in less than half an hour.

Find a piece of board free of knots, about 9 inches wide and $\frac{3}{4}$ of an inch thick. This might be something that started out to be 10-inch shelving; it would have these dimensions when dressed down to surface four sides, or S4S. Cut a piece about 18 inches long. Try to get your end cuts square just for practice.

Measure back $5\frac{1}{2}$ inches from each end, and draw a line across the board at each end, using your try square to make sure the lines are parallel with the ends of the board. Then measure in $2\frac{1}{2}$ inches from each side along these lines, and make a mark. You should have this:

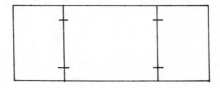

Using your brace and about a 14/16 bit, drill holes at the places where the later marks touch the lines. Remember when using the brace and bit to keep the bit perpendicular to the board in all directions and to stop drilling each hole as soon as the sharp point goes through the board. Then flop the board over and finish the hole from the other side.

Measure in $1\frac{1}{4}$ inches from each end of the board, and draw lines from these marks so that they just graze the holes you have drilled. At this stage, your board will look like this:

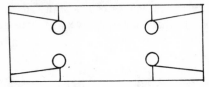

Draw a vertical line between each pair of holes.

Using a compass saw, cut along the lines you drew last.

Then, using a ripsaw, cut along the lines from the end of the board to the holes. If you have drawn good lines and have followed them properly with your saw, you will have this:

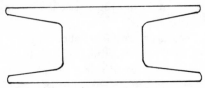

With a wood rasp, or scraper and sandpaper, you can smooth off the rough spots, round the edges, and you will have a very satisfactory reel.

MAKING MODERN PLAQUES

Maybe your house has areas with large blank walls, where you think a plaque would relieve the monotony except that it would cost too much. Here is a very inexpensive answer, and one that gives you an opportunity to try out your artistic sense. If there is some old plywood and paint around the house, it shouldn't cost anything, a fact which is always a consideration.

First, you will need a piece of plywood of any thickness, for the base of the plaque. Cut it to a size and shape that will give nice balance to the space to be brightened, but be sure to cut the corners square—no 85-degree angles, be certain they are all 90 degrees. Start out with squares or oblongs; fancy shapes can come later, after you are sure about consumer acceptance.

Now, using fairly thin plywood (no thicker than $\frac{3}{8}$ of an inch), cut squares, oblongs, triangles, circles, kidney-shaped pieces—any symmetrical shape. Move them around on the base until you get a pleasing design. Imagine how different colors would affect the design.

Sand and trim the plywood until it is as smooth as you can get it. Use plywood filler, and then paint the design in the colors that your own artistic sense suggests.

Glue the small designs to the plywood base. Add a glue-on hanger.

MAKING PLAQUES FOR THE DEN

No doubt on trips to the beach and to the mountains you have seen souvenir plaques, made of a section of log and dressed up with paintings of local scenes. If you have any artistic talent you can make plaques of a much more personalized nature than one that says "Souvenir of Lake Gooney."

Find a log of the proper diameter, and one with good tight bark. Cut it on the bias; in other words, like this:

cut here

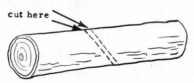

This makes it look like something more than a caveman's idea of a wagon wheel. Sand the cut surfaces just as smooth as you can.

Draw your design on one surface with a soft pencil.

If you have a wood-burning kit, use the tools from it to burn the outlines of the design. If you don't have one, use your ingenuity; gather an assortment of nails (stick them into sections of old broom handles so you don't burn your hands), soldering irons, shish kebab skewers, or other steel objects that will get red hot if you heat them on the stove, and use them to burn in your designs.

Varnish the whole carefully, bark and all, and fasten a brass screw eye to the back. Then bend the screw eye parallel to the wood and hang the plaque up.

MAKING A LOOSE-LEAF BINDER

Occasionally you may want to preserve papers—issues of the school newspaper, for example—that makes too large or too odd-sized a batch to fit in a regular commercial binder. With plywood you can make a very attractive binder that will be something you can show with pride.

Let's say the page size of the school paper is $9\frac{1}{2}$ inches by $12\frac{1}{2}$ inches. Punch holes carefully through the entire file in the left margin, making sure the holes are in a straight line from top to bottom and in the same place on each page. Thus your papers will be in a solid block. If the margin isn't wide enough, paste a strip of paper the same length as the page onto it to widen it.

Take two pieces of plywood, one 10 inches by 13 inches, and one 10 inches *plus the width of the saw kerf* by 13 inches. Using your marking gauge, draw a line along the long dimension of the oversize piece, about $\frac{3}{4}$ of an inch from the edge. Cut along this line.

Attach these two pieces together with small ornamental hinges. Drill holes through the $\frac{3}{4}$-inch strip on one cover and in the same places on the other cover so they line up perfectly with the holes you punched in the paper.

Your hardware dealer will help you select brass bolts, washers and nuts to complete the binder.

Smooth, fill and varnish the plywood to a high gloss. Cut the design from the top of the first page of an extra copy of the newspaper, paste

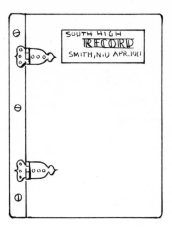

it on the cover carefully, and varnish over it. Put the contents into the binder.

MAKING BOOKSHELVES

Bookshelves are rather expensive. Usually people buy them for a particular room or part of a room, and often they don't look well in another spot. If your family moves often—perhaps because of your father's job—here is a quick, cheap, practical solution to the problem.

By building tiers of loose bricks high enough for the books, and bridging the tiers with shelving, you have quick, flexible bookcases of any size you want.

Use ordinary bricks, which are about $8\frac{1}{4}$ inches long. They are cheap to buy and even cheaper to acquire if you haunt new houses as they are built and ask the contractor to give you the ones he would ordinarily bury with a bulldozer after the job is finished. Often, that really is what happens to the few bricks left over. For shelving, use boards 10 inches wide and 1 inch thick; don't make them longer than 4 feet. Smooth the boards down to S4S. The width will then be $9\frac{1}{2}$ inches and the thickness 25/32 of an inch; that's how much you lose from a standard board when it is smoothed down to S4S.

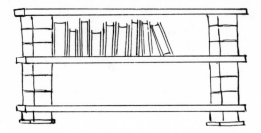

Give the shelving several coats of varnish; this will keep the wood from getting dusty and from tearing the books as they slide in and out of the shelves. Seal the bricks with a clear, invisible waterproofing compound that you can get at good hardware stores. This will prevent the bricks from getting dusty, too.

Cut two pieces of plywood just a trifle larger than the bricks. Place the bottom bricks on the plywood. Then build an even pile of bricks on each side and lay the boards across them. Keep on doing this until you have as many shelves as you want. Don't leave more than 1 foot of space between each wooden shelf, and don't build the shelves more than $4\frac{1}{2}$ feet tall.

MAKING A CARRIER FOR FIREWOOD

When I bring firewood into the house, I usually start out with three or four pieces under my arm. By the time I open and shut the screen door and the outside door, one of the pieces has already dropped and another one is ready to drop at just the right spot to scar a piece of furniture. Naturally the bark is loose and pieces of it fall on the floor, so in the end I have to get out the vacuum cleaner to clean up the mess.

Obviously, it would be better to use a carrier and it's easy to make one. A piece of canvas, about 20 inches by 40 inches, two pieces of 1 inch by 1 inch wood, two short lengths of clothesline, and some nails, and you are well on the way. (These measurements are suggestions.) If you don't want to buy canvas, you might be able to get a piece from an old awning or tarpaulin if it isn't too weatherbeaten.

Cut two sticks so they are $1\frac{1}{2}$ inches longer than the width of the hemmed canvas. Wrap each stick tightly in an end of the canvas, about $1\frac{1}{2}$ times; leave $\frac{3}{4}$ of an inch of stick poking out at each end, so it looks like this:

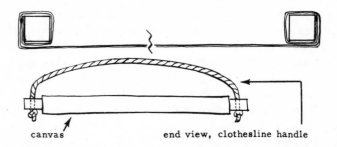

canvas   end view, clothesline handle

Tack the canvas to the wood with any ornamental nails or tacks that take your fancy.

Drill $\frac{1}{2}$-inch holes midway in the exposed portion of each stick at each end. Run clothesline through these holes, knot it so it won't come back through, and you have handles.

FLOORING AN ATTIC

Is your family out of storage space for such things as picnic dishes, the books you had when you were young, the family suitcases, and many other things that winter cold and summer heat won't bother? Is your attic one of those low, unfloored jobs with nothing more than a runway leading to the ventilators? If so, you're the one who can help.

The easiest way to get the additional storage space is to make a wooden floor for the attic. This doesn't involve a lot of precision work, as it used to; after all, all you need is a stable platform for material that is disturbed only once or twice each year.

Haunt your local lumber yards, and let them know you are in the market for defective plywood, $\frac{3}{8}$ of an inch thick or more. You don't care if it is split, or how rough it is; it can't be so bad that it is unusable for this purpose. As you get each piece, lay it *loosely* across the beams and you are in business right away.

47

After you get ten or twelve pieces, 4 inches by 8 inches or even smaller, take the stored material out of the attic long enough to make a wooden floor. Play around with the pieces to get the best possible coverage with the least cutting. There will be posts and chimneys and diagonal braces to cut around, but if you measure well you can fit things rather closely. It doesn't have to be perfect; this is for storage.

Try to match your joints so that if you have to slide something heavy it won't hang up or tear at the joints in the floor. Use 4d nails to hold the plywood to the beams.

There are a few precautions to observe. Be careful not to drive any nails through any wires. Don't lay the plywood over wires that are above the surface of the beams. Don't disturb the insulation between the beams. Watch where you step or you may find yourself with one foot through a bedroom ceiling.

Don't store anything in the attic that will be ruined by heat—no appliances, no Christmas tree lights, nothing with rubber parts. It's wise not to store clothing in the attic either, because it might be damaged by insects.

MAKING A TABLE LAMP

You can make an attractive electric table lamp out of two pieces of firewood. A good clear piece of oak stovewood is the starting point.

Don't make the dimensions too regular; the lamp will lose part of its charm, and might just as well have been made out of pieces from the lumberyard.

For the base of the lamp, saw out a piece of firewood about 7 inches long. If, because of the curvature of the cylindrical log, you end up with a piece that is 5 inches wide at the bottom and 4 inches wide at the top, like this end view, don't worry about it. The irregularity will make the lamp more attractive.

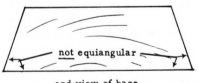

end view of base

The top and bottom, however, and the ends should be parallel.

For the upright portion, saw out a piece about $6\frac{1}{2}$ inches long. Make the ends parallel, but make the rest of it even more irregular than the base. It should taper, so that the top is smaller than the bottom; but do not square it up. It might look like this:

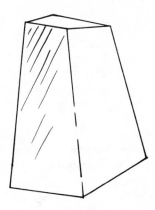

Just don't make any side of the base larger than the width of the top of the base minus a half inch.

Set the top on the center of the base and trace the outline of the top on the base with a pencil. With a sharp wood chisel, carefully cut away the area inside the pencil line. Cut to a depth of about $\frac{1}{8}$ of an inch. The top should fit fairly tightly into the cutout area in the base (hand right but not mallet tight).

Buy some "all-thread," a lightweight threaded pipe, at your electrical supply store. It comes in 3-foot lengths, but some dealers will cut it in shorter lengths for you. You need a piece about 2 inches longer than the upright part of the lamp. It should be of a diameter that will screw into a push-switch socket, which you might as well buy at the same time.

Drill a hole at about the center of the upright, just the right size to fit snugly around the all-thread. Drilling into end grain can be frustrating. The best tool to use would be a drill press if you can get hold of one.

Drill a hole the same size through the base of your lamp, lining up the hole at the place that will make it possible for the all-thread to fit from the upright portion into the base.

Drill a hole about 1¼ inches in diameter from the bottom up to the middle of the base. This 1¼-inch hole will really be a partial widening of the hole that you already drilled through the base. It will allow you room to fit a threaded washer around the all-thread to hold it securely in place.

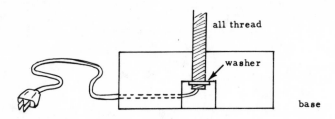

Now drill a ¼-inch hole in the base horizontally. It should join the 1¼-inch hole just below the place where that hole narrows in diameter. This is for the entrance of your lamp cord.

Pull the all-thread through the top and base. Run some electrical wire through the washer and all-thread. Then tighten the washer. Wind on your push-switch socket before you connect the wires at that end. See page 108 for more about wiring. Put a plug on the other end of the wire and then install a bulb. Snap on the type of shade that fits over the bulb with a spring and you have a lamp.

Putting a Finish on Your Lamp. Your lamp is wired and it works but it isn't finished.

Take the lamp apart. Smooth the wood until it is satin smooth, using scrapers, sandpaper (even of 00 grit, the finest grade of sandpaper), and fine steel wool. If there is some wood filler around the house, use it, but it isn't absolutely necessary.

Now on one surface at a time, paint your wood with thin white oil-base interior paint, and quickly wipe it off with a rag. This will leave white paint in the pores of the wood. The raised portions of the wood will retain their natural color. This is what the decorators call "limed oak."

Now you need only apply five or six coats of a good clear varnish, sand lightly with 00 paper between coats, and you should have a good-looking job.

Reassemble the lamp, and admire your handiwork.

PUTTING WHEELS ON CABINETS

Having spent some time in the Army, and a good bit of that time in logistics, I have an obsession about proper storage and cleanliness of storage spaces. I have learned that keeping things up off the ground or floor preserves them from moisture, mildew and insects and that putting shelves and cabinets on wheels makes cleaning easier. All you have to do is move the shelf or cabinet, clean the place where it stood, and roll it back.

Every time I design shelves or a cabinet for use in the basement or garage, I start with the dolly, or roller that it will rest on. Practically all of my dollies consist of a square wooden frame, made of boards 2 inches by 4 inches; in each corner there is a flat-plate chest caster.

Let's take my paint cabinet, for instance. It is a steel cabinet, bought as a clothes wardrobe when my wife and I lived in an apartment. Inside, it's rigged with shelves and racks. It is 20 inches by 20 inches and 5 feet tall. My dolly for this cabinet looks like this:

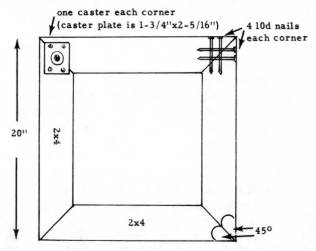

one caster each corner (caster plate is 1-3/4"x2-5/16")

4 10d nails each corner

20"

2x4

2x4

45°

It took me all of thirty minutes to make, using some old 2- by 4-inch scraps left over from another job, sixteen 10d nails, and 4 flat-plate chest casters that cost me a total of 96 cents complete with screws.

One word of caution: do *not* use casters on asphalt tile floors because they sink and dimple the tile.

MAKING A BIRD FEEDER

Aside from the appearance of the finished product, the essential requirements of a bird feeder are three: to be accessible to the birds, to keep the rain and snow off the food, and to keep cats away from the birds.

Here is a quick and easy-to-make bird feeder that will go far toward meeting the requirements.

Take a clean No. 5 or No. 10 can with the top cut out completely. (The school cafeteria or a restaurant will be glad to give you the can.) Using a pair of tin snips, cut as cleanly as possible two lines about 5 inches down from the top edge, about 5 inches apart from each other, like this:

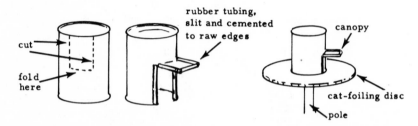

Fold this tab *out* to a 90-degree angle, and round off the corners. Slit a piece of rubber tubing with a sharp knife and cement it to all the raw edges of tin that you have just produced. See the illustration.

If you can't find any used rubber tubing, you can get the same effect with friction tape, but it won't look as well. The important thing is to dull the raw edges to protect the birds and your hands.

With your coping saw, cut a wooden disc that fits snugly into the open top. Nail the can to the disc. With the bottom of the can as the roof, the tab you cut and bent is now a canopy, and the wooden disc is the base.

Place a large disc of sheet metal on the top of a pole and mount the feeder on the sheet metal. The sheet metal will keep away cats.

You can avoid the sharp edges on the cat-keeper-away disc by making a series of $\frac{1}{4}$-inch cuts around the disc about 2 inches apart, and by rolling the edges down with a pair of pliers.

ANOTHER WAY TO MOUNT THE BIRD FEEDER

If the pole and disc method doesn't appeal to you, you can build the feeder as described but fasten the wooden disc in the feeder to a square board or large disc which will serve as a platform for the birds and a place for the overflow of bird seed or suet.

Run an eyebolt through the center of the lid of the can and fasten it with large washers.

What you will have should look like this:

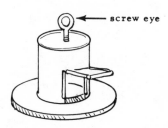

← screw eye

Suspend the feeder from a tree limb or projection of a building, being careful to place it in such a way that athletic cats cannot jump onto it from above.

HANGING A PEGBOARD

You can buy a pegboard of almost any size. Occasionally it's a bit difficult to hang in such a way that the fixtures sold with it and designed to hold things fit into the holes of the pegboard. The problem is to hold the pegboard away from the wall. If it touches the wall, the tips of the fixtures don't have room to go all the way through the holes and then they fall.

The solution to this problem is a type of wooden molding called "backband." It looks like this:

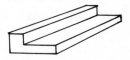

It holds the pegboard just far enough away from the wall.

Try a small piece of pegboard to start with. A piece about 1 foot by 2 feet will make a fine rack for screw drivers and pliers. Buy your backband with a view to avoiding ending up with short pieces. Two pieces of pegboard 1 foot wide and two pieces 2 feet wide will require 6 feet of backband, but you'd better get an 8-foot piece of backband or two 4-foot pieces.

When you get finished, the board in its frame of backband will look like this:

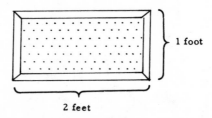

2 feet

You will see that the backband is larger than the pegboard because it extends all around the pegboard like a frame.

Cutting the backband to fit the pegboard is the trickiest part of the operation. You must cut it so that the 2-foot and 1-foot dimensions come exactly at the ridge of the backband rather than at the high edge or the low edge. Use a miter box set at *exactly* 45 degrees and make your first 45-degree cut right at the joint of the ridge. Make sure that each 45-degree angle faces the right way, like this:

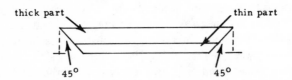

Then fit the pegboard against the backband and mark at the ridge of the backband where the next cut should be. Be sure that the cuts at each end of the backband are not parallel. I lose more wood that way because then I have to get a new piece of backband.

With some very close measuring and eight cuts, your frame should fit. Then screw the pegboard to the backband, using short and thick flatheaded wood screws; start your screw holes with a nail or a hand drill and a very light bit. Use the pegboard holes instead of drilling new holes through the pegboard. About one screw every 8th hole around the edge will give you a tight, rigid frame.

Paint it if you like.

If the wall is cinder block, you can fasten the board to the wall with cement nails. Four will hold it beautifully; drive them through the pegboard holes closest to the edge—in other words, those that are not masked by the wood. Wooden walls are no problem, just nail the pegboard up. If the wall is plaster, use Mollys. Your hardware man can show you how to install with Mollys.

Then buy your pegboard fixtures (their screw-driver holders come in many sizes) and the job is done.

MAKING A WASTEBASKET

Ice cream is delivered to stores in 5- and 10-gallon paper drums. With a bit of fast talking you might possibly get one or more of these away from the source of your banana splits, and your wastebasket will already be well on the way to completion.

Clean it thoroughly. Paint the inside with your favorite color. This is difficult to do because of the shape; you will have to use a paintbrush with a very short handle and even so you will probably end up with paint on your elbows and in your armpits.

Decorate the wastebasket with colored pictures, taken from almost any source, depending on your hobbies and interests. Some of the best decorations I have seen were cutouts from automobile sales brochures, acquired by a foot-wearying round of visits to new car dealers. Another eye-catcher was decorated with the covers from popular magazines on science and mechanics. One would-be football center decorated his wastebasket with color pictures of particularly appetizing dishes from his mother's homemaking magazines.

Paste the pictures to make a neat and symmetrical design. Put a shellac finish over them.

Taking Care of the Family Car

Minor automobile repairs often cause trouble and cost more than they seem worth when you have them done in repair shops. This chapter describes several preventive measures and a few minor repairs which you can perform yourself.

The projects in this section are jobs any reliable person can do, but it is important to do them right. The family car is no object for hit-or-miss, lackadaisical attention. Mistakes or carelessness here can cause accidents, breakdowns in traffic, or just plain expense.

Many of the projects can be carried out by younger members of the family. Talk things over with your family and discuss which responsibilities each member will take before you start. If you are fussy about your car you had better make sure that each person has a complete understanding of his job before work is begun.

KEEPING A MAINTENANCE RECORD

One of the simplest things you can do for the family car is to keep a maintenance record. This will be a reminder of needed service.

If the car still has its *Owner's Guide*, you can probably get the information for your chart from that. If not, a dealer who sells your make of car undoubtedly has a chart hanging on the wall of his service department. Use it as a guide. Your chart may look like this:

Service	1,000	2,000	3,000	4,000	5,000 (up to 50,000)
Lubrication (Every 1,000 miles)	X	X	X	/	/
Tune-up (Every 5,000 miles)					/
Check brakes (Every 5,000 miles)					/
Check front end (Every 5,000 miles)					/
Rotate tires (Every 5,000 miles)					/
Adjust steering gear (Every 10,000 miles)					
Drain and flush transmission (Every 10,000 miles)					
Repack front wheel bearings (Every 10,000 miles)					
Inspect brake linings (Every 15,000 miles)					
Replace oil filter element (Every 4,000 miles)				/	
Drain and replace oil (Every 2,000 miles)		X		/	

This chart indicates that the car has gone more than 3,000 miles, but less than 4,000 miles. Mark one line in the square to indicate when the work *should* be done and another line crossing the first one when the work *is* done.

Draw your chart carefully on a large sheet of cardboard, and fasten it to the garage or basement wall. You must keep it up-to-date at all times; just a week of putting off marking the chart and you may forget important information.

KEEPING TIRE PRESSURE AT THE RIGHT LEVEL

When cars travel, the tires get hot; the pressure inside the tires builds up because heat causes the air inside them to expand. The tire pressure has already increased by the time it is checked at the gas station because the car had to travel to get there. This means that there is more pressure than if the tires were cold. The attendant at the gas station adds less air, therefore, than the tires really require.

Insufficient pressure in the tires causes extra wear on the sides of the tread; but even greater damage results from the fact that the walls of the tires keep flexing more than they should. This builds up intolerable heat and causes the tires to wear out much sooner than they would normally.

If you get a tire gauge to use at home, you can check the tires' pressure while the tires are still cold, and then the driver of the car can ask for the proper amount of air at the gas station. Tire gauges cost anywhere from 89 cents to $3.95. Find out what pressure the manufacturer of your family car recommends, and remember that the recommended pressure is *always* the pressure when the tires are cold. To use the gauge, first unscrew the valve cap on the tire. If there is no valve cap, make sure you get one. They're important. Put the gauge over the valve quickly, before much air escapes from the tire. If you do this properly, there will be just one "phsst" and the bar on the gauge will move out. Then make your reading.

CHECKING THE OIL, LIGHTS AND BATTERY

The Oil. As soon as the family car begins to be the old family car, you can expect it to use up lots of oil. Some attendants at gas stations are a bit careless about checking oil, especially at night when the light is bad. You can save the family a lot of trouble if you check the oil regularly—once every three days or possibly more often, depending on how much the car is used.

To check the oil, pull out the dip stick and clean it off thoroughly with a paper towel. Then put the dip stick back in *all the way* and pull it out again. See how high up the film of oil clings to the stick. If you are doubtful about the reading you got, take one again. Occasionally the oil is so clean you have difficulty reading the dip stick. Not all dip sticks read the same, but most have a line that reads "Add Oil."

Keep a supply of oil in the garage or in the house, and find a system for adding it. My system is to buy oil in 10-quart cans; I pour it from the can into a 1-quart bottle that looks like a round milk bottle with a spout on it and I use the 1-quart bottle to pour oil into the crankcase. One of my neighbors buys his oil in 1-quart cans and uses a service station pourer-opener that he bought at an auto supply store. Whatever your method, the trick is *not* to get more oil into the crankcase than is necessary to reach the "Full" mark. Too much oil is harmful as well as wasteful.

Be sure to put the oil filler cap back on the car after you have added the oil. It's easy to forget to do it and messy when you forget. It's even worse to leave the cap on the motor, where it can short the ignition or fall into the fan.

The Lights. It's a rare driver who doesn't get caught at one time or another with a light out on his car. A driver can go on for weeks without knowing that some of his lights are not operating until he hears the policeman's siren. A weekly check of the lights might save you from a fine or an accident.

Turn on the lights at low beam. Walk all around; check both tail-lights and both headlights. Step on the floor switch, and check the high beam. Also check the back-up and parking lights.

Unless you have someone to help you, stop lights are difficult to check. Turn off all the lights; it's best to do this in the dark. Prop a large reflecting surface about 6 feet behind the car—a large mirror, a big sheet of white plywood, or anything that will reflect light. Step on the brake pedal, and make sure you see *two* spots of red light in your rear-view mirror.

While you're at it, try the horn, and if you have permission to start the motor, test the windshield wipers, too.

The Battery. For some reason people who check their cars thoroughly for most things never remember to check the level of fluid in the battery. In hot weather especially, batteries lose fluid rather fast. Some attendants at gas stations forget to check the battery; it should be done every time the driver stops the car for gas or oil. Batteries are expensive, and operating without the proper level of fluid ruins them fast.

Unscrew the caps of each cell. Look into the cells. You will see a star or circle or some other mark a fraction of an inch below the cap. The fluid should be up to the level of this mark *but no higher*.

If the level of fluid is low, most city water is satisfactory for batteries. There are a few places, however, where the water contains harmful chemicals. Find out from your service station if the water in your neighborhood is bad enough to require the use of distilled water in batteries.

Don't try to pour water out of a pitcher or other container. You can't control the flow accurately enough and you'll splash water on the battery. You will need a battery-filling syringe, which you can get at auto supply stores for less than a dollar.

"OPERATION TIGHTEN-UP"

In cities where cab drivers own their own vehicles, you can often see them, while they are waiting for a call, going over their cabs with a screw driver and wrench, tightening body screws and bolts. This constant care stops rattles and squeaks, and makes even an old car sound good.

Start on the inside of the car. Use the *proper* tool: a Phillips screw driver for Phillips screws, and a screw driver *that fits* for the ordinary type of screw. You can do more damage than good with the wrong screw driver. Tighten every screw you find except those that have anything to do with the motor. Changing the adjustments on the carburetor, for instance, could cause trouble.

Be sure the tool is placed properly in the slot, and work from an angle that will prevent the tool from slipping out of the slot. After you finish with the screws, do the same thing for all the bolts you can find and reach except those that have anything to do with the motor. The proper size of wrench can save you bruised knuckles as well as rounded corners on the bolts. If the wrench is too large and slips around the bolt, it will round off the sharp corners on the bolt head, making it impossible to tighten the bolt and difficult to remove it. If you don't have a wrench that fits, don't try it.

WASHING THE CAR

Since everybody knows how to wash a car better than anyone else but waits for somebody else to do the job, the boy of the family usually ends up doing it, with plenty of advice from the sidelines. The only way to discourage the chorus of advisers is to know how to do it better than they do. There are as many "*don'ts*" as there are "*do's*" in this job.

Don't wash the car in the hot sun. You can wash it in the shade no matter how hot it is. Washing in the sun makes for a streaky job, and can even break down the finish because of the sudden cooling effected by the water.

Don't use hot water. It dulls the finish.

Don't use soap or detergents if the car is waxed or polished, because they remove the wax or polish.

Don't use a stiff brush on anything except the tires. It scratches the finish.

Don't start the job until you are sure all the windows and ventilators are closed; water-spotted interiors will not raise your popularity rating. You can do the job with a hose and a rag. I prefer a mitt that has a sponge rubber pad attached; in the pad there is a tube that connects to the end of the hose. A gadget that many people like is a metal tube ending in a brush (some have a whirling brush, turned by the water stream). I find these difficult to use because it is hard to keep the stream of water steady, but there are those who recommend them highly.

Start at the top and work down. After you have gone over the body of the car, look over the job carefully. If you find "holidays," or places you have missed, go over them again. If the car has been to the beach or in slush, give the undersides of the fenders a good dousing with a strong hose stream.

You will probably find spots from spilled gasoline, road tar, and other things. Your thumb nail will take care of some of them. A *light* washing with detergent and a rinse *immediately* after you have gotten a spot clean will take care of most of the rest. On really stubborn tar stains, try a little kerosene; use detergent afterward to get rid of the kerosene and then rinse with water. Wax or polish the places where you used detergent.

Clean the tires with a stiff brush and detergent. A little elbow grease will bring out the really black color of good rubber. The whitewall area will come clean with steel wool pads or a regular whitewall cleaner.

The easiest way to wash the windows (and *please* do the insides as well as the outsides) is to use paper towels. First use a wet towel on an area about half the size of the windshield. Follow this with a dry towel to pick up the rest of the dirt and to dry the glass thoroughly. And roll the windows down to get the part that slides into the top of the door. Most boys miss that area.

Look over the chrome carefully, especially the area where the tail pipe comes closest to the bumper. Where you see rust or stain, use a wet rubber chrome cleaner; it looks like a huge pencil eraser. A little elbow-bending here makes all the difference in the world.

Give the inside of the car a good going-over with a vacuum cleaner. Use the paper-towel system on the dashboard and especially the glass on the dashboard. Empty the ash trays, and don't forget to dust off the rear window ledge.

MARKING YOUR LUG WRENCH

Most people sooner or later buy a 4-way lug wrench. It makes sense because you can get better leverage with it, loosen the lug nuts more easily, or tighten them more securely.

What doesn't make sense is the way the person changing the tire has to continue to try all four openings to see which one fits the lug nuts on his car, not only every time he works on a wheel, but also every time he puts the wrench down to pick up another lug nut.

Fit the wrench to the lug nuts on your car and paint the proper socket on the wrench the same color as the car. If you have two cars of different colors and with lug nuts of different sizes, paint each socket of the wrench the same color as the car that it fits. When you get new cars, remove the old colors and start over again.

It will save you time and frustration and only takes a few minutes.

CHANGING A TIRE

When people talk about changing a tire, they actually mean changing a wheel. Because of the way modern automobile tires and wheels are made, taking a tire off a wheel and putting it back on again requires several hundred dollars' worth of power equipment or the strength of a Hercules.

Changing a wheel is a dangerous pastime, now that the design of automobile underbodies and chassis requires the use of a bumper jack instead of an old-fashioned frame jack. *Bumper jacks are dangerous!* Trust them about as much as you would a rattlesnake. Several tons of automobile landing on you suddenly is not recommended for your health, so be very careful when using a bumper jack. If your bumper jack is as junky as most that come with today's cars, try to talk the family treasurer into buying a tripod jack with a screw drive instead of a ratchet drive. They cost about $6.00 and are much safer and simpler to operate.

There are times when it is necessary to change a wheel, and you might as well be prepared to do it when you can't call the motor club. I suggest very strongly that, if you are going to use an ordinary bumper jack, you know what you are doing before you try it yourself. Read the following instructions carefully.

First, if possible, place the car so the flat tire is away from traffic. If this isn't possible, have someone guard you with a bright-colored cloth, to caution and slow down approaching traffic. At night, use a safety flare. You have a right to insist before the occasion arises that the family keep three or four flares in the trunk of the car. They cost less than a dollar each.

Second, if the right front tire is flat, place a stout piece of wood or a fair-sized stone *behind* the left rear wheel. If the right rear tire is flat, put the wood or stone in *front* of the left front. The jack not only lifts, it also has a tendency to push the car away from it. A piece of lumber 4 inches by 4 inches, cut as in the illustration, is a good thing to keep in the trunk for use as a block.

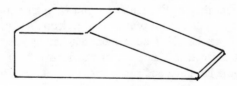

There are many styles of jacks; with a bit of forethought you can figure out how the one that comes with the car should work. Try it out both up and down, turning the ratchet lever to reverse direction. Work the lifter on the jack to a position just under the bumper. Working from the outside, position the jack so that it is fairly snug against the bumper guard. This means, for instance, that if you are jacking the left front tire, the jack should be on the left side of the left front bumper guard. If you are jacking the right rear tire, the jack should be on the right side of the right rear bumper guard, as in the illustration.

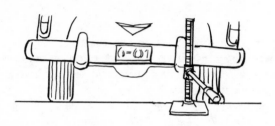

Before you actually lift the car, but after the jack is snug against the bumper, remove the hub cap or wheel cover. Be careful not to bend or mar the cap. You might find a depression in which a screw driver or the sharp end of your lug wrench will fit; use the tool for leverage in prying off the hub cap. If there is no such depression, fit the screw driver or the sharp end of the lug wrench into the joint between the hub cap and wheel, and tap it smartly.

Now, while the wheel is on the ground, loosen the lug nuts a turn or two, but no more. You should be using the weight of the car to hold the wheel still while you tug at the lug nuts. When you have the nuts loose enough so that they don't require too much tugging (but *not* so loose that you can turn them with your fingers) jack up the car high enough to clear the flat tire. Jack it up a few more notches, because the spare with air in it will be larger in diameter than the flat tire.

Take off the lug nuts, and put them in the hub cap so you can find them when you need them. Remove the flat.

Bring up the spare. Lifting the wheel and tire from a cramped position and positioning it on the lug bolts is a very tough physical feat. As an alternative, you can place the tire on a thick board and slide the board with the tire on it into position (see page 63). This might require a bit of fancy jack work, but it's worth it. The car has to be in a position that will permit the lug bolts to slide right into the holes in the spare wheel. A few notches either way on the jack will do it.

Even service station men commit the sin of tightening up the lug nuts in a manner that puts the wheel on in an off-center position. It takes only a minute or two to do it right. Put each nut on finger-tight. Now, when you tighten the nuts with your lug wrench, don't tighten each nut as tight as you can and then go on to the next one. Instead, tighten the first one fairly tight. Then choose one of the two as far away from that one as you can, and tighten it to about the same tension. Work around the wheel, *never* tightening two adjoining lug nuts to the same tension, but rather pairs of lug nuts on opposite sides of the wheel. This will make the wheel go on straight.

If you are working on a front wheel, have someone hold his foot on the brake; this will give you some resistance to work against while you are tightening the nuts. For rear wheels, this is unnecessary because presumably the parking brake, parking gear or both have already been set.

Don't bother to put the hub cap back on; you might scar it. Put it in the trunk along with the flat tire and all the tools you used.

MAKING A GUIDE FOR PUTTING THE CAR IN THE GARAGE

Is your car a tight fit in the garage? Does Mother have problems getting the car far enough into the garage so the doors can be closed but not so far that she bumps into the wall? Is the space for the car narrow because of lawnmowers and barbecue grills stored along the side? You can really help on this one!

Park the car in the garage just exactly where it should be.

Get a brightly colored sponge rubber ball. Drive a hole through the center with a large nail. Get some kite string and tie a button on one end of it. Thread the other end of the string through the ball; use a darning needle if necessary. The button will keep the string from coming all the way through the ball.

Then hold the string up to the garage ceiling; move it around until you find the point where the ball at the other end just touches the front of the ornament on the car. Mark that spot on the ceiling. Drive a staple into that spot, but not all the way in. Run your string through the staple; tie it just high enough so the ball rests on the hood ornament.

Now all the driver has to do to get the car into the right place in the garage is to aim for the ball and stop when it touches the hood ornament.

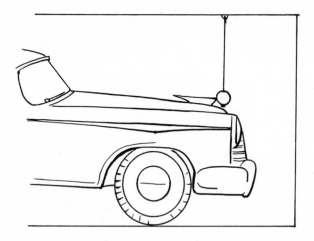

GETTING RID OF GREASE SPOTS ON THE GARAGE FLOOR OR DRIVEWAY

Almost any car that has been around a while will drip oil and grease. If it is kept in the garage or a pavement driveway, someone is sure to step in the grease and then track it in on the carpets in the house.

A weekly scrubbing of the floor or driveway with a grease solvent will keep Mother on your team. You can buy a can of grease solvent at a gas station or auto supply store. All you have to do is follow the directions on the can.

Taking Care of the Lawn, Garden and House Plants

In most families there is at least one person who enjoys working in the garden. Often it is Mother or Dad, but when they get thrown off schedule for one reason or another, it is often the younger members of the family who must pitch in. Gardening can really be fun for the whole family.

This section offers a few hints for successful gardening. If this sort of work appeals to you, look in a good gardening encyclopedia for more hints. Remember as you try to apply the suggestions here that different climates and types of soil may require different techniques.

WATERING THE LAWN

Probably more lawns are ruined by poor watering practices than by any other cause.

A little water is worse than no water. Don't even start the job unless the ground is going to be drenched, and wet down to a couple of inches below the surface. Light watering causes the roots of grass to turn up and become shallow. A good watering once a week does a lot of good, while a light watering daily or every few days does a lot of harm. The idea that watering during the day is harmful has been pretty well discredited. It is better to water in the hot sun than not to water at all.

Holding a hose for a little while is fun, but not if you hold it long enough to do a proper job. There are many styles of sprinklers—

rotaries, oscillators, pierced hoses and seeping hoses. Use what you have because almost any kind will do the job if you take the trouble to become familiar with its capabilities. Rotaries sprinkle over a round area and oscillators sprinkle over a square-shaped area. Pierced hoses can take care of a long line of shrubs or bushes and seeping hoses get the water into the ground faster.

Small trees and shrubs, especially newly planted ones, are best watered by placing a hose without a nozzle several inches away from the trunk, on the side where the ground is higher, and letting just a trickle run for hour after hour. This gets the water down to the roots.

GIVING A PLANT A LONG DRINK

Sometimes people are hesitant about taking week-long vacations because they are afraid their house plants will die from lack of water while they are away. Here is a solution that often works. Try it out before you go away, and prove to yourself that it will do the job.

Fill a bucket or other container with water. Then cut or tear a strip of flannel or similar material, long enough to reach from the bottom of the bucket to the plant. Tie one end around a weight and put it in the bottom of the bucket; wrap the other end around the plant stalk or pin it to the dirt with toothpicks. Keep the bucket on a lower surface than the plant.

The cloth strip will act as a wick and will keep the dirt in the pot moist.

CUTTING THE GRASS WITH A ROTARY MOWER

There are probably more rotary gasoline mowers in use these days than any other kind, even though they are more dangerous than other types because of the high speed of the blades and the possibility of accidentally sticking a foot under the shell.

There are a few safety precautions to observe.

Keep your feet out from under the mower when you are pulling the starting cord.

Take every step as if someone were lurking behind you ready to kick your foot into the mower. On terraces and other grades, be sure that the grass gives you a firm footing; if possible walk off to one side of the mower rather than directly behind it. If you have football shoes, wear them; they give you firm footing and the cleats will open the soil and allow air into it. If the terrace is especially steep and long, rig up a rope harness and let the mower down from the top by the rope. With a little practice you will be cutting the grass effectively on both the drop and the recovery.

Be careful that there are no stones or other foreign objects in the path of the mower. A spinning blade hitting a rock can throw pieces several city lots away, and any person who intercepts a piece of rock or metal flying at high speed can be killed or severely injured. It has happened.

When you stop the mower, pull the spark-plug lead. This way you can be *sure* the mower won't start unexpectedly.

Now let's go on to getting the job done. The lawn will look better from the street if you make your cuts parallel with the street rather than vertical to it. On the other hand, the most efficient method of cutting a large area is to run one continuous cut along the outside perimeter of the yard's longest oblong or square, continuing the cut right inside of the first one, and so on until you finish at the center. Using this system, you do less switching of the mower; just make 90-degree turns and it's almost like making one long cut in a straight line.

If the grass is too tall and the motor begins to stall, either move more slowly or lift the mower on its back wheels until the motor begins to pick up revolutions, or do both. A bit of alertness here will prevent a lot of pulling on the starter rope.

When a tree or plant is in the path of your cut, come up to the tree, back off and make a half-circle around it. When you arrive at the other side of the tree you will be facing the direction from which you started. Drag the mower *backward* until you have enough room for the handle and yourself to turn around without interfering with the tree. Then turn around and move on.

If you have a wire fence and want to get as close to it as possible, pull the mower *backward* along it. You can get much closer that way without digging into the fence.

When you have finished cutting the grass, turn the mower off and take a few minutes to clean the grass out of the mower. It will be easier than waiting until after the grass dries and becomes a solid, matted mass.

Check your oil every time you use the mower, and check your air filter at least every fourth time you mow the lawn.

If starting becomes hard, remove the spark plug and have your local service station clean it and gap it; you can look up the proper gap in the instruction booklet that came with the mower.

Have a specialist in lawn mowers sharpen the blade and clean the carburetor at least once every season.

When you put up the mower for the winter, remove *all* the gasoline; it gets gummy and plugs things up if you leave it in the mower over the winter. Also, remove the oil.

EDGING THE LAWN

Probably nothing you can do with a lawn will give you so much effect for so few blisters as the job of edging. Grass grows sideways as well as up, causing untidy borders along the sidewalks and curbs. There are many styles of lawn edgers on the market, ranging from electric and gasoline-powered jobs to hand edgers. If you don't have a real lawn edger, you can do the job with one of those long-handled ice scrapers.

Edging with hand tools is really a hard job, so don't try to do it all at once. A schedule of as little as 10 feet a day until the job is done breaks it down into chunks that don't seem too formidable, so you won't be discouraged before you start.

TAKING CARE OF GARDEN TOOLS

When the family gardener decides to go out and help Nature, it takes the wind right out of him (or her) not to be able to find the garden tools at all, or else to find them mud-encrusted, dull where they should be sharp, and generally not fit for the job.

The best time to clean a garden tool is right after you have used it, before the dirt gets encrusted and the rust embedded. Water and a stick will take the dirt off; drying in the sun or with a rag, and then a light coating of oil will do the rest of the cleaning job.

If you wait too long, the job gets harder. A long soaking and the use of a blunt stick together with plenty of elbow grease will bring a lot of improvement. Then you will have to follow this by using files, steel wool, and wire brushes. When you get all of the dirt and most of the rust out of the tools, oil them lightly and remember for the next time how much easier it would be to clean them right away after use.

Sharp-edged tools should be kept sharp. It is much easier to take a few minutes to file an edge on a spade, for instance, than to ruin your shoes, back and temper trying to drive a dull spade into stubborn earth. Use a fairly fine file for sharpening. *Don't* sharpen spades, shovels and hoes with an emery wheel. It gets the tools too hot and makes them lose their hardness and toughness and become permanently dull much more quickly.

If you don't know what kind of an edge to put on your garden tools, talk it over with your garden supply man or better yet, look at the tools of a good landscape man to see how the edges should look. Be sure to take out any nicks; these are the sign of a sloppy workman.

Do *not* try to sharpen scissor-like tools, such as hedge clippers, pruning shears and the like. There is a definite technique to sharpening these gadgets, and amateurs can create more damage than an expert can repair. Even though you can't sharpen them, be sure that they are clean, free of rust, and lightly oiled.

If there are small children around, sharp-edged garden tools can cause accidents, even when they are stored. Make a guard for the tools by taking a discarded garden hose, cut a piece of it off, and split the piece lengthwise. Be sure it is a little longer than the edge of the tool. The natural spring in the hose will hold it in place over the sharp edge, and it's easy to remove. (See illustration on next page.)

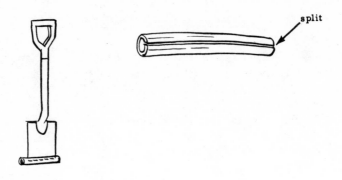

split

Look at the handles every so often. Rough places will appear in even the best of them; light sandpaper will save blisters.

There should be a 20-yard penalty for any person using a tool handle as a poker in a bonfire. For some reason this is a temptation hard to resist.

HANGING GARDEN TOOLS

No garden tool should rest on the floor. Every one of them should hang from the wall. That old joke about stepping on the tines of the rake and having the handle hit you on the head isn't really very funny.

It's so easy to hang them that it's a shame not to do it. All you need is some wall space, a 2-by-6 board long enough to hold the tools, a few nails to hang the board to the wall, and a handful of 10d common nails and finishing nails to hang the tools from.

If you are attaching the board to walls of cinder block, use cement nails. If the board is to go against a wooden wall, be sure you nail it to the heavy studs, and not to light sheathing. Remember that garden tools are heavy, and you will need plenty of nails to make the board secure enough to hold a good deal of weight.

When the board is up, it is time to fit your tools to the board. If space is at a premium (and it usually is), try to arrange the tools so that a short one and a long one alternate. My board looks like this:

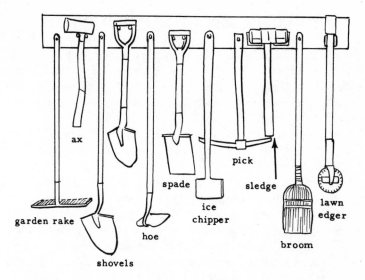

ax

spade

pick

sledge

garden rake

ice chipper

hoe

lawn edger

broom

shovels

For tools with D-shaped handles or other projections from which you can hang them, use 10d common nails. For tools like rakes and long-handled shovels, drill holes in the handles for the nails to pass through, and then use 10d finishing nails. With a bit of ingenuity you can figure out a way of hanging almost anything. My own ingenuity has been stymied only by a garden spreader with a single handle, but I look at it every week or so and I have faith that I'll work it out yet.

In the illustration, note that the lawn edger was hung with a spring clip designed for hanging brooms and that the sledge hammer was hung on two 90-degree-angle mending plates, with an end of each one turned up just a bit to keep the sledge head from slipping out. Certain other tools may require tricks like this, but get them off the floor.

Be sure to hang sharp-edged and pointed tools so the edge or point faces the wall rather than out into the room. This is a safety measure that is easy to forget.

After you have taken the tools down to use, you may forget which one belongs where. So with a grease pencil, mark at each place the name of the tool that belongs there. This is also a useful system for learning quickly which tool is missing; then you can retrieve it from the yard before one of the neighbor's kids falls on it and gets hurt, or before the rain gets it rusty.

SORTING OUT GARDEN SPRAYS AND SPRAYERS

If more than one person in your family works in the garden, it's a sure bet that the sprays and insecticides are jumbled helter-skelter, and that the spoons, pans and other measuring and mixing devices are in sad shape. You can do everyone concerned a good turn by bringing some system into the situation.

Many a plant has died because weed killer got mixed with the bug killers. Many a dollar has been wasted because the buyer didn't read the label before he bought.

Spread out on the cellar floor all the bug killers, the weed killers, the spray guns, and the measuring spoons and pans. See what you have. You will be astonished at how many of the same things are there. Four different rose sprays? Even different brands may use the same active ingredient. What does the label say about the formulas? If two of them are of the same formula, place them on the shelves so the package with less in it is in front of the other one.

Separate the weed killers from the bug killers. Find out if one of the sprayers is earmarked for specific uses; Dad may have meant the bucket-sprayer for weed killers, and Mother uses it for bug killers; no wonder the azaleas died! Label the sprayers as to their uses on a card, and shellac the card to the sprayer. Do the same with the pans or pots that are used for mixing. Wire the spoons to the proper pans even if you have to drill a hole through the handle to do so.

If you have shelf space, mark the top or bottom of each section of shelf with what is placed there, such as Rose Dust, Rose Spray, Rhododendron Food, Fungicides and so forth.

Put all the things on high shelves, where the younger kids can't reach them too easily.

Tricks for Easier Home Maintenance

Things do go wrong around the house, some of which must be fixed, and many of which can be prevented. This section contains a sampling of ideas that might make it easier for you to keep things going more smoothly.

KEEPING A NOTEBOOK OF INSTRUCTIONS FOR APPLIANCES

Almost all appliances and gadgets from lawn spreaders to clothes-drying racks come with instruction books, lists of parts, guarantees, or all three. But when something goes wrong, the whole family has to search for the instructions, and the likelihood of their being found is usually very slim.

There is an easy way to solve this problem, and you can be the family hero by taking charge.

Get an inexpensive, thick 3-ring binder, $8\frac{1}{2}$ inches by 11 inches. Get some paper to fit it and a stapler.

Collect all the instructions that can be found around the house. Attach them to the paper with the stapler or punch three holes in the instructions themselves, if they come on large enough sheets.

File them alphabetically in the notebook binder and make an index, leaving blank lines for new additions. Keep the book in a spot where it can be found when needed, and insist that anyone who uses it put it back in the same place.

This will save the whole family frustration, time and expense.

MAKING A SCHEDULE FOR CARE OF THE FURNACE

Most modern furnaces, using forced air, require a certain amount of care. The filters should be changed once a year or oftener if they get *very* dirty, and the motor and fan bearings should be lubricated once a month.

The trouble is, of course, that nobody knows when the job was done last. This is a very simple problem to solve.

Just draw yourself a form like the one in the illustration. Staple it to a piece of stiff cardboard or glue it to a piece of light plywood and hang it near the furnace, near enough to be a reminder, but not near enough to catch on fire.

FURNACE-CARE RECORD
1961—1962

Date	Lube Motor	Lube Fan Bearings	Replace Filter	Vacuum Filter
Sept. 30	X	X	X	
Oct. 30	X	X		X
Nov. 30	X	X		X
Dec. 30	X	X		X
Jan. 30	X	X		X
Feb. 28	X	X	X	
March 30	X	X		X
April 30	X	X		X
May 30	X	X		X
June 30				X

TAKING CARE OF ELECTRIC FANS

In many households, when the central heating goes on the fans are put in the attic—"period." Comes the first hot day next spring, and there is a gooey, oily mess to clean up before the fans can be used.

Clean the fans thoroughly *before* you put them away. Use a rag that's slightly moist with kerosene to take off the film of lubricating oil from the blades and the rest of the fan. Don't bend the blades while you are cleaning them, and be extra careful to pull the plug out before you start the job at all.

Don't oil the fans before you put them away.

After the fans are as clean as you can get them, protect them by careful wrapping. If they fit into large grocery bags, wrap them this way, and staple or tape the opening to keep out the dust. If they are too large for grocery bags, try one of the thin plastic bags that cleaners use. Just wrap the fans as airtight as you can.

Comes spring, rip off the bag, give the motor a few drops of oil, and enjoy the breeze.

During the season when you use the fan, keep it cleaned and oiled. Too much oil is harmful; if you can't find the instruction book that tells you how much oil your particular fan requires, use five or six drops of SAE 20 auto oil (light, summer oil). It is better to oil the fan with a few drops regularly than to drown it in oil once a year.

If the fan develops vibration, pull the shaft back and forth to see if there is excessive play. If so, there is probably a bearing that needs to be replaced. Take the fan to your repairman because the chances of your finding the right bearing for replacement are very slim. The vibration might also come from a bent blade rather than from a faulty bearing. To find the bent blade, you can hold a piece of soft white chalk lightly but firmly in front of the blades, and then turn the blades by hand to see which one doesn't touch the chalk at all or touches it too hard. Another way of finding the bent blade is to run the fan electrically, looking down on it from the top to see if one blade makes a pattern different from the others.

ADJUSTING THE DOORS OF BUILT-IN CABINETS

Perhaps by now you're tired of hearing older people say, "They don't build things the way they used to." This was never truer than when said of doors on built-in cabinets. The carpenters are often very careless about the placement of hinges and catches, with the result that some of the doors are always popping open.

You can fix them. The first thing is the "diagnosis," as the doctors say. Is it merely a matter of moving the catch inside the cabinet so that it meets the prong on the door? This is often easy since you will find that, by backing off the screws a few turns, the screw holes in the catch are elongated and give you a few 16ths of an inch of room to play with.

Move the catch in the proper direction and then tighten the screws. If you cannot get into the cabinet to see from the inside in which direction the catch needs to be moved, you can accomplish the same result another way; rig a pencil or crayon on the prong of the door so it will make a mark as the door closes.

If the catch is too far off for mere adjustment to take care of the difficulty, you will have to use a different method. Take out the screws, plug up the screw holes by driving in wooden matchsticks, and start new holes in the proper place with a hand drill and a bit about half the diameter of the screw. To get the matchsticks even with the door surface, start with a sharp knife, progress to a rasp, and finish with sandpaper. If you do your "matchsticking" properly, you may be able to drive the new screw into part of the old hole without difficulty.

Occasionally the trouble is not in the placement of the catches, but is caused by improper hanging of the door itself. This is the problem if the door doesn't even close properly, binding above or below. Here is another case that calls for removing screws and plugging holes. Before you do it, though, figure out which way you want to move the hinges and how far. It often works out just the reverse of the way you think it does at first. It's often helpful to remove only one hinge and then hold the hinge with one hand, the door with the other, and a pencil with a third hand (belonging to the helper you'll need for this operation). When you have the door at the proper angle to fit, mark the outline of the hinge *and the screw holes in the hinge*. Plug the old holes, drill new ones, and tighten up. You might have to move both hinges.

UNSTICKING A DOOR

Doors that stick, especially the ones inside the house, are often very easy to fix without planing or scraping. This won't work every time, but it works often enough to try it first.

Doors usually stick at the top, but no matter where the door scrapes, look the situation over carefully and ask yourself if moving one of the hinges away from the door jamb (not the door) just a trifle might ease the situation. Remember that if you move the top of the door in one direction the bottom will move in the opposite direction.

After you have figured out whether it's the bottom or top hinge that needs moving, unscrew the hinge at the jamb side and back it up with a piece of cardboard. If the door is eased some but not enough, use more cardboard. You might even have to cut a piece of very light wood (such as you find used in baskets) as a shim. A shim is a thin piece of wood, metal or other material used to fill up an unwanted space.

Occasionally the trouble is not in sagging hinges, but in a change in the actual shape of the doorway. Here is a real problem, and if the change is too great the only solution is to call in a good carpenter. But if the change necessitates trimming the door only $\frac{1}{4}$ of an inch or less, you

can do it yourself with a rasp or block plane. If you use the rasp, hold it in both hands and keep it level so that you won't round the top of the door—a thing that's very easy to do, especially when you don't want to. If you use the block plane, remember never to run it off the edge of the door; you will take a big chip of door along with the plane. If you have to trim the edge, always work from the edge in, not from the inside out to the edge.

When you get to that point where the door is sticking just a little bit, and you're not sure exactly where the door and jamb are touching, rub some colored chalk on the jamb, and close the door. The high part of the door will pick up the chalk, and show you exactly where to trim some more.

REPAIRING WARPED STEPS

Wooden steps outdoors tend to warp and settle. Often the result is that water gathers in the trough left by the warping or in the angle between the tread and the riser. In case you didn't know, the tread is the part you step on, and the riser is the part that leads from the top of one tread to the bottom of the next one. Water remaining on the wood causes the wood to rot. Even worse, in winter the water turns to ice and causes accidents.

If the steps have merely settled, you can probably lift them with an old-fashioned automobile jack (*not* a bumper jack) until they are at the proper angle once more, and prop them in place with bricks and/or wooden shims.

If they have warped or have settled past the point where they can be jacked and propped, drill some holes straight through the wood. Make them about $\frac{3}{8}$ of an inch in diameter at the lowest point in the warped portion. Then the water can drain off.

UNSTICKING WINDOWS

There are two principal types of windows, and both can cause trouble by sticking. Casement windows, the kind that swing out when you turn a crank, develop two kinds of difficulties, and both are simple to fix. Often the handles are very hard to turn or simply won't budge. This is almost always a matter of lubrication. With a screw driver and a bit of observation, you can remove the crank assembly and figure out where to lubricate. Some automobile cup grease (a special, heavy grease) or even petroleum jelly in a pinch, applied with a knife blade or spatula, will do the job. After you have applied the lubricant and before you tighten everything back together, swing the window back and forth with your hand (not with the crank) to get all the rubbing surfaces free and lubricated.

Occasionally the upper portion of the window will bind against some portion of the window assembly. Work the window back and forth until you know exactly where it is binding, and then file (for steel casements) or plane or rasp (for wood casements) just enough to obtain the necessary clearance. After you file, plane or rasp, remember to paint the surface to protect it.

Double-hung windows, the kind that slide up and down, can be a real problem if they become rebellious. First, you have to diagnose the trouble.

If the problem is merely paint on a place on the sash, where there shouldn't be any paint, you can often solve it by running a thin-bladed tool between the binding parts and scraping or cutting off the unnecessary paint. You will probably have to do this both from inside and outside the house. If this doesn't solve the problem, it requires some real carpentry, and I recommend that you call in a carpenter.

CAULKING

Caulking is the putty-like compound applied around window and door frames to make a tight and somewhat flexible seal between the frame and the wall. Since it is usually painted to match the rest of the window trim, many home owners don't even know it is there. Most houses that are more than a few years old suffer from acute "draftitis" around window frames and door frames because the caulking has dried and shrunk. It may even have fallen out.

To make the fuel bill go down and the comfort of the house go up, you will need a caulking gun and some caulking compound. The caulking gun and the compound look like this:

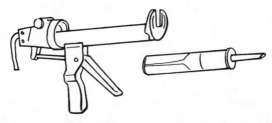

The gun costs about $2.50; the compound is about 50 cents a cartridge. Guns have improved lately; the new open-frame type shown here is much easier to clean than the old closed-frame type. With the older type, it took more time to clean out the dried compound from the gun than to do the caulking. Buy cartridges with tubes already on them.

With a hooked scraper, which you can make yourself, or an old worn-out screw driver, remove the dried-up caulking from around the frame as best you can. The cleaner you make the frame, the better the job will be.

Put the tube of compound in place in the gun, move the nozzle end of it along the frame, and squeeze the trigger. If you squeeze too fast, you'll have to move the nozzle fast to keep the compound from piling up. With a few false passes, and a bit of patience, you'll pick up skill quickly, and soon be getting a smooth, ribbon-like joint of uniform thickness. Just remember that caulking compound is designed to stick to almost any surface and it's very difficult to remove, even from your hands. So try to get it all in the place where it's supposed to go. If the caulking doesn't lie smooth, you can fix it with a putty-knife or other tool, but dip it first in linseed oil.

CHECKING THE WINDOW SCREENS

If there is a room in your house in which turning on a light at night is an invitation to thousands of flying visitors, and if you can't find any holes in the screen itself, there are several checks you can make.

Darken the room and have someone with a pencil-shaped flashlight run the light around the outside rim of the screen. If you see light from the inside, then there is an opening in the rim of the screen. You may be able to close it merely by repositioning the screen. Or possibly the screen is placed properly, but not held firmly enough against the window frame; in that case tighten up the screws in the clips that hold the screens.

Once in a great while you may find that the screw in the clip will not turn all the way, or that the hole for the screw has been positioned wrong. This means either retapping the hole that wasn't tapped properly in the first place, or drilling a new hole in the proper spot and tapping it. You need a tap wrench to retap the hole. Most hardware dealers will lend or rent out tap wrenches since householders have so little use for them. You will have to buy a die, which is the tool you need to cut the threads in the hole, that is, the ridges corresponding to the ones on the screw. Take the screw from the casement clip with you, so the dealer can help you select the proper size drill bit for the hole or the proper size and thread for the tap wrench and die.

FIXING SCREEN DOORS THAT SAG

Sooner or later most screen doors will begin to bind at the bottom. Cutting them down with a plane isn't the right solution because this leaves a gap at the top.

At the hardware store you can buy a turnbuckle, a tool designed for just this problem. At each end of the turnbuckle is a piece of heavy wire with a loop at the end. The turnbuckle comes complete with screws to fasten the loop to the frame of the door.

Put the turnbuckle on the door in the proper direction so that when you tighten it, it will lift the corner that binds. Figure things out for a moment or two before you begin to drill holes for the screws. It's very easy to put the turnbuckle on backwards and this will make the trouble worse instead of better.

Don't turn the turnbuckle any tighter than necessary to free the sticking portion of the door. There's no point in setting up unnecessary strains on the door.

And while you're at it, let the hardware dealer show you some of his "non-slam" door closers or cushions—hydraulic, pneumatic, or compression-spring type. Dad would appreciate not hearing the door slam, but he probably just never got around to doing anything about it.

PRESERVING SCREEN DOORS

Is there a small child or a dog who opens the screen door by pushing against the bottom of the screen? Admittedly, the best way to take care of this would be to teach them better, but an easier way is to protect the screen against their best (or worst) efforts.

Cover the bottom part of the door with hardware cloth, a very strong mesh that comes in different sizes and that will protect the screen without cutting down on the circulation of air. You can tell very quickly which side of the door to put the hardware cloth on; put it on the

concave side of the abused screen, since that is the side the push is coming from.

MAKING SCREENS FOR WINDOWS

You can make a satisfactory wooden-framed screen to fit almost any open space, from a basement window to an entire porch. Of course, if you intend to screen a porch, it will take several or many panels, but the principle is the same.

Start with a screen for a simple window. Measure the inside dimension of the window opening carefully. Use a try square to check the corners; chances are they are not exactly square and your screen will have to be a slightly irregular, four-sided figure instead of a perfect rectangle. At this point decide whether you think it's better to make a perfect rectangle that might fit on three sides, but will fit the fourth only with some planing, or to try to make the frame slightly irregular so that it will fit all four sides of the window opening without any planing. I have found that this second choice is usually a losing battle, and it's simpler in the long run to plane the fourth side to fit.

Make up your bill of materials. The window opening, let us say, is 35 inches long by 22 inches wide. Double these and add them together, and you get 114 inches. The most economical piece of lumber to buy (if you are using $1'' \times 2''$ lumber) would be a 10-foot, or 120-inch piece. With only 6 inches to spare you can't waste any, so be careful and work precisely. Buy the same length of half round $\frac{3}{8}$ of an inch wide; you won't need quite as much half round as the other lumber but an 8-foot length v n't be enough. For a window opening this size, buy 2 feet of 36-inch screening or 3 feet of 24-inch screening. It doesn't make much difference, as you can see.

Now cut off one end of your 1″×2″ board. Saw it off straight instead of the cockeyed way it came from the lumberyard. Mark it carefully with your try square, and follow the lines with your saw. Measure *exactly* the 35 inches for the length, mark it square, saw carefully, and hope it fits the opening snugly but without force. If it is a bit too long you may be able to trim it down with a block plane; if it is more than ⅛ of an inch too short, you might as well try another cut from the original board, and hope to salvage this one for one of the 22-inch cuts for the width. Using the same procedure, saw your other three pieces— one more 35-inch piece and two 22-inch pieces. As you cut each piece to fit, mark it with a pencil so you know whether it is top, bottom, or left or right side.

When you have all four pieces to fit the window opening, it is time to fasten them into a frame. I recommend that you use an end-lap joint; it's the simplest to make and is as strong as any. The end lap looks like this:

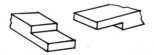

To make it, cross the end of one 1″×2″ board perpendicular to the end of another, like this:

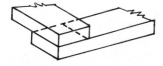

Draw a straight line across the bottom piece, using the top piece as a guide. The two pieces must form a perfect right angle and must be exactly flush with one another on the outer edges. With your marking gauge, mark a line lengthwise along both edges of the bottom piece, bisecting the thickness of the piece, like this:

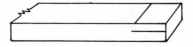

85

Drop a line from the pencil line vertically to the marking gauge line on both sides and pencil in the marking gauge line. Mark "X's" so you will not become confused about which piece is to be discarded, and which saved.

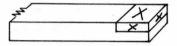

Now, with a miter box and backsaw, remove the pieces marked by the "X's." Be careful to take the lap out of the same surface at both ends of the same "stick," like this:

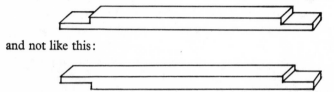

and not like this:

Square your cut with a sharp chisel, since for some reason the saw never quite makes a square cut from the end grain into the line previously cut across the grain. Put your frame together before nailing it, to test for the fit of the joints. If there are round spots or other imperfections, take them out carefully with the chisel, until the joints fit properly.

Once you are satisfied with the fit, tack the frame together lightly with small finishing nails; test it frequently with the try square to be certain that the frame is either square at every corner or off-square at the points where you want it that way.

After you have tacked the frame with the light nails, drill two $\frac{1}{16}$-inch holes about $\frac{1}{2}$ inch in from each corner for screws; one hole should be on top and one at the bottom, like this:

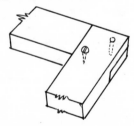

Then put in the screws.

Now try the frame in the opening for fit. Adjust it with your plane where necessary. Once you have the kind of fit you want, you will have to figure out your own system for holding the screen in place. Then give the frame a prime coat of thin white paint. When the prime coat dries, give the frame a coat of final color also. Paint the half round at the same time.

Now comes the next precision step—measuring and cutting the screen mesh. Measure the *inside* dimensions of the screen frame, and add $\frac{1}{2}$ inch for overlap to both the length and width. Look at the illustration:

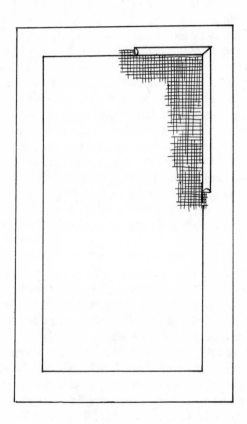

Using $\frac{3}{8}$-inch half round, you can conceal the overlap with the half round by cutting the screen mesh so it also overlaps $\frac{1}{4}$ of an inch. The mesh will still be $\frac{1}{8}$ of an inch shorter than the outside dimensions of the half round, like this:

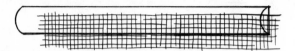

The drawing is made as if the half round were glass or plastic, so you can see the mesh under it.

Cut the screen mesh with tin snips or a very sharp knife; the knife is better if you have a sure hand and a steel straightedge. Place the screen mesh over the frame so it covers the wood by $\frac{1}{4}$ of an inch in every direction. If you doubt your eye, draw the $\frac{1}{4}$-line on the wood so you will know you are right. Drive the mesh into the frame with a carpet tack, starting in an upper corner. Drive tacks every $2\frac{1}{2}$ inches around the frame, keeping the wire stretched as you go. The tighter the stretch is, the better the job will be. If your fingers aren't strong enough, stretch the mesh with a pair of pliers, padding the jaws first with adhesive tape. If you see the mesh beginning to wrinkle or ripple, pull out the last tacks you drove in and stretch the wire by pulling on it, at right angles; then tack it down again. You may ruin the first piece of mesh while trying to get it just right, but with practice you will be able to get the mesh stretched on a screen frame so tight it will sound like a drum if you thump it.

You might find it best to tack one long side and one short side first, then start down the other long side. Start tacking from the remaining short side about 6 inches from the end, changing the direction of pull as you go, and alternating to prevent ripples. After a few trials you may even find a better method of your own.

Now cut your half round. Cut a 45-degree angle at one end, using a miter box. Even the 50-cent kind of miter box will do. Measure the inside dimension of the frame for the particular side or end you are about to cover. Measure your half round from the short side of the 45-degree cut; this will be the short side of the next cut also, as shown in the illustration:

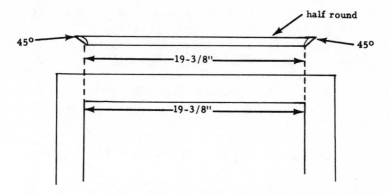

Tack down the half round with 2d finishing nails, and repeat the entire operation around the frame. If you have measured everything right and tacked the screen properly, the half round should cover all the raw edges of wire mesh, and you will have a workmanlike job.

SCREENING A PORCH

Screening an entire porch is quite an undertaking and not to be entered into lightly. You can do it, though, if you take the time to do it right, and if you remember that the job is basically one of making several or many screens, making them larger than window screens, and making the frames into which they fit.

Get someone who knows about screening porches to help you figure out the largest screens you can make with the kind of wire mesh available, the amount of work space you have, and the length of your own arms. Panels larger than 4 feet wide and 8 feet long are unwieldy and very difficult to make. I wouldn't try them myself.

From this point on, it is basically a matter of your using $2'' \times 2''$ or $2'' \times 4''$ boards as uprights that will hold the screen panels as you make them. If the roof of the porch is very high, make horizontal frames to go between the uprights; this will shorten each screen panel to a length you can handle with greater ease.

On the *outside* of the uprights and the horizontal framing pieces, nail $1'' \times 2''$ boards so you will prevent the screen from falling out and

89

to add extra protection against the entrance of insects. Use screen door hooks to hold the screens firmly against the 1-inch by 2-inch stops. It is best not to nail the screens in permanently; you will want to take them out for cleaning, painting and repairing.

As the crowning touch, buy duplicate sets of numbered nails. Place one nail on the lower left corner of each screen and its duplicate number nearby on the frame. If you take the screens out for any purpose, you will always know then where each one fits.

TAKING CARE OF GUTTERS AND LEADERS

Most householders neglect the gutters under the eaves that carry rain water to the ground. When these gutters become plugged with leaves or other debris the water has to go somewhere, so it usually ends up coursing down the walls. This causes damp walls inside the rooms, and the walls become damaged from falling plaster.

The gutters should be swept out at least once a year to get rid of the accumulation of trash. If your house is low enough so you can safely use the ladders on hand, you can do this yourself.

After sweeping, check for rust. Brush it away and then repaint the gutter. At your paint store you can get special paints for the insides of gutters that protect them from rust and that are not very difficult to apply. Gutters are very expensive to replace so it is worth while to take care of them.

The leaders are a bit trickier to check (leaders are sometimes called downspouts). You can look them over on the outside for broken and rusty spots, and you can drop an 8-ounce fishing sinker, tied to a string of course, down through the pipe, to make sure it's open.

PREVENTING LIQUIDS FROM FREEZING IN THE WINTER

If you live in an area where zero or subzero weather occurs almost every winter, give some thought to freeze-prevention before the thermometer is scheduled to take a nose dive.

Outside faucets will freeze if it gets cold enough, and that can necessitate expensive repairs later. You can prevent them from freezing by shutting off the line to the faucets, using the valve inside the house. Then open the faucets and let them drain. You haven't done yourself a bit of good unless you let them drain, because the water that's already in the faucets will remain there and will of course expand as it freezes.

Move outboard motors, garden hoses and other items that are likely to retain water into the basement or into other warmed and protected areas. Take your insecticides and other liquids with a water base inside. If there is a possibility of water remaining in the sprayers, move them inside also.

If your dairy doesn't supply boxes to hold deliveries of milk, make one. You don't even need a hinged top; you can make the top separate and put a weight on it to hold it firmly in place. Make it of $7'' \times 8''$ boards. If the weather gets really cold, line the box with insulating wallboard. If you like ice caps on your milk bottles, don't bother at all.

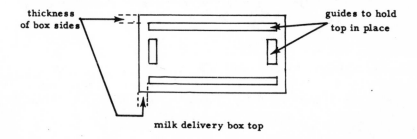

thickness of box sides

guides to hold top in place

milk delivery box top

MOUNTING THINGS IN PLASTER

If there is any job women give to handy men that can cause said handy men to take up crocheting, it is fastening things to plaster walls. The walls become ruined from unsightly cracks and even missing chunks of plaster. Fastenings fall out, and the thing that's supposed to hang on the wall winds up on the floor instead. Plaster just wasn't made to hang things on, but mothers often become adamant.

If a small, lightweight picture is to be hung, the new adhesive hangers are probably the best bet. Buy the size suited to the weight of the picture, follow directions, and hope it works.

If the thing to be hung seems too heavy for an adhesive hanger, or even if you're putting up a small spice rack, the so-called picture hangers, consisting of a light-gauge brass nail leading through a brass hanger, are more advisable. Get the right size for the weight of the object (plus a safety margin), and protect the plaster by first putting a piece of sticky cellophane tape over the spot where the nail will enter. The cellophane tape doesn't always work, but it works often enough to be worth the try.

Some things to be fastened to plaster, like paper dispensers and curtain rods, get a certain amount of outward pull in addition to the downward pull of the weight of the object. Here is where you breathe a deep sigh and talk it over with your hardware dealer. Tell him the problem; he will offer several possible solutions, including Molly screw anchors and split-wing toggle bolts. My favorites are Mollys, and I use them every time I have a choice.

Be sure when you buy Mollys that you get the instruction sheet from the dealer and a Molly wrench. Mollys of different sizes require drill bits of different sizes. Do not try to use a Molly unless you have the proper size of bit for your drill; you can learn the size from the instruction sheet.

Even Mollys can get you into trouble, however; they require a hollow place behind the plaster, and if you happen to drill your starting hole in a place where there is a stud or a shoulder in the cinder block, the only thing you can do is start over again and repair the first hole.

Taking Care of the Plumbing and Heating

Because of the complexity of modern plumbing and heating systems, home mechanics have been relegated to the sidelines in these fields. The new faucets are so complicated and so covered with chrome that the amateur can do more harm than good even in trying to replace simple things like washers. There are so few activities left for the do-it-yourselfer that they can be covered in a very short section.

FINDING THE MAIN SHUT-OFF VALVE, OR "OPERATION RED HANDLE"

When plumbing troubles hit, like a burst pipe or a jammed valve, it's too late to go looking for the shut-off valve. Beat trouble to the punch.

Find the place where your water supply line comes into the house. Very close to the entrance point there is a valve. This is the main shut-off valve; turning it in the proper direction shuts off the flow of water into the house.

PAINT IT RED! That will make it easy to find in an emergency.

If plumbers who cared worked on your house, there may be other shut-off valves to block off water to specific parts of the house. Paint these red also, and make a chart showing which valve controls each set of plumbing fixtures.

UNPLUGGING DRAINS

When the kitchen or bathroom sink drain doesn't drain at all or drains very slowly, you can come to the rescue.

The first thing to try is a "plumber's friend," or rubber force cup. Put it over the drain. Run water slowly into the sink. If there is an overflow drain, hold a hand over that so you don't lose your suction. Work the force cup up and down, being sure it covers the drain opening. In many cases the vacuum created is enough to loosen whatever is plugging the pipes. Complete the job by running a half-package of baking soda and hot water down the drain. The baking soda will dissolve the grease. In fact it is a good idea to run baking soda and hot water down the drain every few weeks just as a preventive.

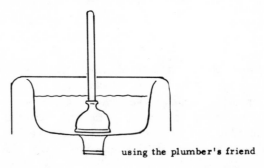

using the plumber's friend

If the force cup didn't do the trick, the next step is to check the trap. This is the curved portion of the drain under the sink. Before you work on the trap, remember that there is always water in it. Put a pan or a bucket under it before you open it so you'll catch the water instead of Mother's wrath. Traps in older houses often have clean-out plugs at the bottom of the curve. With this type it is quite easy to unscrew the plug and clean out the trap with a wire.

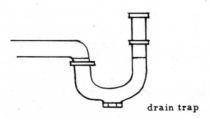

drain trap

If there is no clean-out plug, you must take off the trap itself. You do this by loosening the two large nuts, and the trap comes off entirely. Get the goo out of it and put it back together again *carefully*. Be ever so cautious about cross-threading; don't force things. If the trap leaks slightly after you get it together, and you are sure you have threaded the nuts properly, you can stop the leak temporarily by plugging it with heavy laundry soap.

MORE ON UNPLUGGING DRAINS: USING THE "SNAKE"

If the force cup doesn't clear the drain, and if opening the trap doesn't do it either, the trouble is probably below the trap. This calls for a "snake," called in the catalogues a "drain and trap auger." It looks like this:

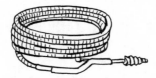

Set the handle a couple of feet from the working end. Insert the working end into the pipe, and using the curved handle, keep turning the snake until it goes well into the pipe. Loosen the set screw on the snake, bring your handle back a foot or two, tighten the set screw, and twist some more, all in the same direction. When this much goes down the pipe, repeat the procedure, loosen the handle, bring it back a foot or two, tighten the set screw, and turn the snake some more.

As the snake reaches bends in the pipe it may become stubborn, but if you keep turning it, the entire length will gradually go down the drain. When it goes all the way, run some water through. If the pipe drains, turn the snake a few more times for luck, and then, still turning in the same direction, pull it out of the drain.

If it works, use some baking soda and hot water to complete the job.

If it doesn't work, the job is bigger than both of us, and it's time to call the plumber.

The snake is the proper tool for clearing a toilet bowl also. Insert it into the hole in the toilet bowl and repeat the same procedure as described above.

THAWING FROZEN PIPES

One thing to remember, if you have a frozen pipe in your house, is that pipes don't usually break when they freeze; they break if the ice inside them thaws abruptly.

First inspect the pipe as well as you can for breaks. If it is broken, close the nearest shut-off valve and call the plumber.

If you think the pipe is not broken, start thawing it with no more violent means than hot, wet rags. Blowtorches and electric heating gadgets are for the experts, who have had experience at this sort of thing. Don't use candles either. Have somebody stand by ready to close the shut-off valve in case there is a break after all.

Keep the faucet open, so the water that comes from the melted ice will have somewhere to go. Once it begins to run, let it run until you are sure all the slush has passed through.

FIXING TOILET TANKS THAT DRIP

The toilet tank that won't shut off or that continues to drip is both a waster of water and an annoying noisemaker. It is usually so easy to fix that it is difficult to understand why most families put up with this type of trouble.

Let's take a look at the drawing:

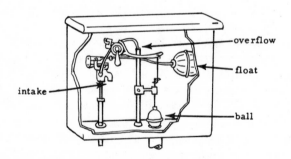

toilet tank diagram

More often than not, the trouble is in the ball that fits into the hole at the bottom. If it is more than a few years old, replace it even if it looks all right. These balls are cheap (about 50 cents or less; about 75 cents with guide and brass rod). Shut off the water at the valve below the tank. Unhook the rod that goes through the ball from the lever that holds it, and unscrew the ball. Screw on the new one. Hook it up again. Open the shut-off valve. Chances are your troubles are over.

Occasionally the ball may be all right, but the rod doesn't hold it in the right place. Flush a few times while you observe the action, and you should be able to see if the rod needs straightening and in what direction.

Once in a great while the float valve, actuated by the copper float on top, doesn't shut off properly. The tip-off here is water in motion in the bowl after the float has reached the top position. If this is the case, and if the shut-off isn't working, water is going down through the overflow. This calls for replacing the washer in the float valve, which is a bit complicated. For this I recommend a plumber.

If you happen to live in a place where water is very expensive or has to be trucked in, you will want to adjust your float so that the tank doesn't get very full, since the tank needn't be full for the toilet to flush properly. You can regulate the amount of water entering the tank by adjusting the screw on the float valve, or if it has no adjustment screw, by bending the float-valve rod. In some areas you can save a wad of money by experimenting until you permit the tank to fill up just enough to flush properly.

FIXING LEAKY FAUCETS

Many years ago, replacing a faucet washer to stop an annoying drip or leak was fairly easy. If your house has the older type of faucet, you too can replace the washer easily. First, shut off the valve below the faucet. If your house doesn't have a shut-off valve for each faucet, shut off the main intake valve. In either case be sure the valve is shut off; you can tell that it is when you turn on the faucet and no more water comes out of it.

Wrap the cap nut with adhesive tape or a rag to protect the finish, and turn it counterclockwise. Next, unscrew the valve stem from the faucet by turning it counterclockwise also. Take it out.

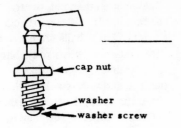

cap nut

washer
washer screw

The little washer at the bottom of the valve stem is the troublemaker. Carefully loosen the screw that holds it. Replace the old washer with a new one of the same size, which you can buy at any hardware store. If the screw is corroded, replace that also.

Assemble the faucet in reverse order from the way you disassembled it, and turn the cap nut just tight enough to stop any leakage around the valve stem.

If this treatment did the trick, take a bow. If the faucet still leaks, then the valve seat is probably worn out, and it's time to call the plumber.

Some faucets, particularly those in laundry tubs, are packed with graphite-impregnated yarn. Occasionally this packing works loose, with the result that the upper part of the faucet leaks. You can buy new packing to replace it. Just note how it fits in as you disassemble the faucet.

If you live in a very modern house, the faucets are undoubtedly so complicated that you will have to call the plumber when they leak. After ruining the chrome on my kitchen faucets, I have decided that the only faucets I will try to repair hereafter are those in the laundry tubs and the outside faucets for the garden hoses.

If you feel you must work on the modern chrome gadgets, watch the plumber while he does it, and note carefully the tools he uses.

FIXING CLOGGED GARBAGE DISPOSALS

Don't try to repair a garbage disposal unit without having the accompanying instruction booklet on hand. If you can't find that booklet, write to the service manager of the company that made it, asking for a replacement booklet; in your letter, tell him the model number and other data you may find on the serial-number plate riveted to the under-sink unit.

Before you get too familiar with a disposal unit, remember that this machine cannot tell the difference between your fingers and food scraps! Be *certain* that the switch is turned *off* before you stick your hand or anything else into the unit; warn everyone else around also not to turn the switch on while you are working.

Some disposals have water switches. These are additional safety devices that prevent the motor from turning until there is a sufficient stream of water passing through the unit. Often these water switches get out of adjustment. A little study of the adjusting screw and some help from the person who uses the disposal most will enable you to readjust it. Have your helper run the cold water at the rate that works best, while you turn the screw to the point where the unit shuts off. Then turn it back an eighth of a turn at a time until it allows through the minimum stream of water the unit needs to run.

Occasionally the unit will just stop. If it has a re-set button (which is red), wait three minutes, punch the re-set button and hope that the unit starts. If this doesn't work, turn the unit off at the switch. Using a stout stick 2 or 2½ feet long, turn the base plate a quarter turn to the left or right, according to the accompanying instruction booklet. Turn on the switch and try again.

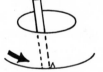

rotating disposal base plate

If this method doesn't work either, check the fuse that controls the disposal. If the fuse is burned out, replace it (see page 110). If none of these methods work—a new fuse, the quarter turn of the base plate, and pushing the re-set button—call the repair man.

WHAT TO DO ABOUT GAS LEAKS

I do not recommend that do-it-yourselfers, even adult ones, fool around with household gas. If you suspect something is wrong, call your gas company.

If you smell gas, cut off all the fires you can, shut off nearby electrical equipment that can throw sparks, and open the doors and windows. Don't let a concentration of gas build up. Caution people about lighting matches or smoking.

If you feel you must find the leak, *do not* try to find it with a match or lighted candle. You might find it and go up in flames simultaneously. You may use a flashlight and a bowl of sudsy water. The flashlight is safer than a light with an extension cord, which might spark. The sudsy water will help show you where the leak is because it will bubble if it gets very close to the leak.

You might be able to make a very temporary repair with a paste made of laundry soap moistened with water, but don't count on it to hold more than a little while, just until the gas man arrives. The soap patch might hold better if you wind a rag or adhesive tape around it. Even chewed chewing gum, held on with a rag, might hold the leak for a while.

SAVING FUEL

In almost any house, it's natural to grumble about the big gas or coal or oil bill. Also in almost any house a few simple tricks can save an appreciable amount of fuel.

One door, left open to the outside for one minute, will lower the temperature of the average-sized house one degree. Convince the younger kids that leaving doors open while the furnace is running cuts down on hamburger money.

One of the greatest thieves of household heat is an open damper in the fireplace. Most families are reluctant to close the damper because it is so easy to forget that it is closed and to go ahead and start a fire anyway; then smoke fills the house. Make a simple signal to inform whoever makes fires about whether the damper is open or closed. Take a wooden strip about 2 inches wide and a foot long. Paint one side white, the other red. Prop it in the fireplace with the red side showing when the damper is closed, the white side when it is open. And of course take it out of the fireplace when a fire is burning. Even if the stick gets turned when it shouldn't, or doesn't get turned when it should, its presence will still be a reminder to check the damper.

Leaky windows also make the fuel bill go up. You can plug up the leaks with weatherstripping. There are many different kinds for different kinds of windows; ask your hardware dealer about what kind to use on your type of window. Choose one that's easy to apply. Buy only enough for one window at first so you can see if it applies as easily as the advertising claims it does.

Leaky basement doors cause loss of heat, too. Often they are short for their frames because they must open inward against a concrete floor with a downward slant for drainage purposes. A piece of rubber matting or old stair carpeting, tacked to the underside of the door, will adjust to the slant as the door is opened and give a good seal when it is closed.

Check your attic floor to be sure it is insulated. If it isn't, there are many kinds of insulation to use. The easiest kind comes in the form of bats, or pads; you just lay the bats between the beams. The granular form is also easy to use, but if there is much wind in the attic it might not be satisfactory. A good insulation job will cost money even if you do it yourself.

With hot-air heating systems, many houses have "cold zones" that tempt the occupants to raise the thermostat instead of balancing the heating system. Remove the case from the heaters in the hotter rooms. The space between the two pieces of sheet metal that you see there regulates the amount of heat coming into the rooms. If you bend them closer together, the space narrows and less heat enters the room. Conversely, if you bend them farther apart, the space widens and more heat comes in.

If you find cracks that are not part of a door or window opening, you can't use weatherstripping. Get a small package of a special putty-like filler that comes in coils, and plug the crack with it.

At night fresh-air fiends should close their doors while the windows are open.

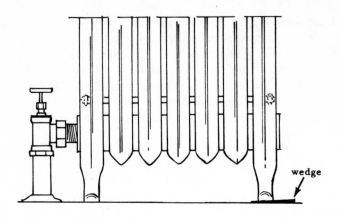

wedge

FIXING LEAKY AND NOISY RADIATORS

If your home is heated by hot-water heat, you should make it your duty to check the water level in the system. If the water level is not kept up properly, some rather inconvenient things can result. The least that can happen is that the radiators on the upper floors of the house will remain cold because the water cannot get to them. The worst that can happen is an explosion caused by the little bit of water remaining in the pipes being converted to steam. In between is another expensive problem: burned-out water jackets in the furnace.

The gauge in the hot-water system is always above the topmost radiator in the house. Check it at least once monthly—oftener if the water level seems to require it. The filler valve for bringing the water in the system up to the right level is often near the gauge.

During the heating season open the vents in hot-water radiators about every 15 days to let the air out. The space taken up by air in the radiators contributes nothing to heating the room. When you open the vent, be sure that you have a bucket or other container under it to catch the water that will also come out. When you open the vent, the hiss you hear is the escaping air. Let the air escape until water begins to drip, then shut off the vent. If the gauge shows that the radiator is full of water, but no water comes out of the radiator and it doesn't heat, it's time to call the heating man.

If the valve on your steam radiator goes bad, buy a new one and replace it.

Watch the water gauge on your steam system even more closely than you would on a hot-water system. If the water level is very low, don't add cold water while the system is hot; cold water poured onto hot metal causes breaks in the metal. Let the fire go down before you add the water.

Steam radiators have automatic air valves, and the fact that they hiss and blow shouldn't bother you. If the radiator bangs, it's fairly easy to make a fix that usually works. Just slide a wedge under the end of the radiator away from the inlet pipe. Make it about $\frac{1}{2}$ inch thick at the thicker end, as thin as you can at the thin end, and about 4 inches long. Slide the wedge in only far enough to stop the noise.

Household Electricity

Many people believe that the best thing to do about household electricity is to leave it alone. This is not a casual fear. Electricity in household voltages can be very dangerous if not treated with proper respect. The trouble is, some people are so afraid of electricity that they don't get closely enough acquainted with it to learn the real dangers.

However, if you are careful and have some knowledge, there is really no reason why you cannot slowly learn more about electricity and save yourself electrician bills while protecting your home from possible fires and dangerous situations. It is important to develop confidence while working with household electricity, but *never* get careless.

FINDING THE MAIN SWITCH

There are many types of fuse boxes in homes, and to draw diagrams of them all would clutter up this book. Have someone who *knows* what he is doing show you how to pull the main switch, that is, the one that stops *all* current from coming into the house. It's too late to learn where this is when there is a real emergency. Knowing how to pull this switch may save a life or a house. If you never learn another thing about electricity, learn this important safety measure.

If someone gets an electric shock and is unable to let go of the wires or appliance, *don't* grab him with your hands. You might suffer the same fate. Pull the main switch. Ditto if a short circuit is shooting off sparks or flame. This is no time to try to find out which circuit is involved. Pull the main switch.

LEARNING SOME BASIC ELECTRICAL TERMS

Most American homes work on 110-volt or 120-volt, 60-cycle alternating current. Now what are we talking about?

Let's think of electricity as if it were water coming through a pipe.

Volts. This is the pressure behind the "water"; it's the force that makes it shoot through a sprinkler or that carries it up to the top of a large building. A volt is the unit of measurement of this force. Volts are named for an Italian scientist, Alessandro Volta.

Amps. The real word is *ampere*, named after a French scientist, André Ampère. This is the unit of measurement of the amount of "water" going through the pipe. If the pipe is large, it will carry more "water" at the same pressure than if it were small. Since the pressure in the home remains constant at 110 (or 120) volts, a big motor or an electric iron will take more amps than a light bulb.

Watts. This is the unit of measurement of the work the "water" can do. The pressure (volts) times the amount of "water" (amps) determines the amount of work the "water" can do. Watts are named for an English scientist, James Watt.

Kilowatts. The prefix "kilo" means 1000 in the metric system of measuring things. A kilometer is 1000 meters; a kilogram is 1000 grams; similarly, a kilowatt is 1000 watts.

Kilowatt-hour. This is the amount of work that can be done by one kilowatt in one hour. Your electric bill is based on kilowatt-hours. The more kilowatt-hours you use per month, the bigger the monthly bill. This is why you should turn off the lights you are not using.

Cycles. In alternating current, the kind almost all homes use these days, the direction of the current changes a certain fixed number of times each second. In 60-cycle current, the current changes direction 120 times a second, or a complete turn-around 60 times a second. The accuracy of the electric clocks in your home depends on the accuracy of the number of cycles at the generating plant. If the master clock in the power company were off one cycle in 60, your electric clocks would lose one minute every hour. Appliances are usually designed for a specific cyclic rate. Appliances designed for foreign countries with different cyclic rates may burn up if used with American current. When you buy secondhand appliances, be sure to look at the manufacturer's plate and see that they match the current in your house.

220-Volt Service. If three wires come off the pole into your house, you undoubtedly have 220-volt service. This is usually stepped down through your fuse box so that you are still getting 110-volt current at the outlets. Certain heavy appliances, however, like stoves and air-conditioners, may be getting the full 220 volts. Be careful with these. Most 220-volt wall outlets have holes for three prongs (one is a ground) but you can't be sure. Get some expert help if you find this type of outlet.

Direct Current. Direct current does not change direction. A few neighborhoods still have it, but it is going out fast. Some bargain-priced used appliances were designed for direct current, and become useless in an area of AC current. Look at the manufacturer's plate when you buy used appliances. Direct current is more costly to transmit over long distances, but it is fine for streetcars, elevators and other machines using variable-speed motors.

The Mathematics of It. We said above that volts times amps equals watts. This means also that watts divided by amps equals volts. Or watts divided by volts equals amps. This isn't merely an exercise in arithmetic. It's pretty important. If the plate on your dehumidifier cleaner reads: "115 v. 500 w." and you want to know if you can use it on a 15-amp circuit that is already carrying 10 amps, you must translate that "watts" to "amps." Dividing 500 by 115, you get very close to 4.4 amps, which still offers a little margin for safety.

BASIC ELECTRICAL THEORY

Don't let this mouthful of terms frighten you. It's really very simple. We keep talking about electrical "circuits." This gives you a hint that we're talking about a circle. Electricity that is produced by the generator at the power station must make the complete circuit back to the generator, and usually does so through the ground.

Look at the illustration below:

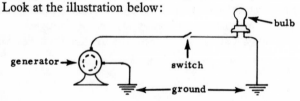

When the switch is closed (and a switch is merely a gadget for holding electrical contacts apart when we want to and touching them together when we want to), the current flows through the wires to the bulb, makes it light up, and then flows to the ground. The switch is *closed* when it is turned on, and *open* when it is turned off.

Now look at the next illustration. Note that the wires at the bulb are touching; there is a *short circuit*. This is what blows fuses and causes fires. Instead of traveling through the resistance of the bulb, the current goes straight through to the ground.

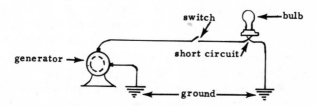

Electricity always follows the path of least resistance. Since it is easier for the current to by-pass the bulb, it does so. So much current is drawn through this easy path that the wires get hot, something burns, or somebody may even get electrocuted. Short circuits are real trouble.

There is a safety device that *usually* can prevent a short circuit from causing too much damage. This is a fuse. Look at the next illustration.

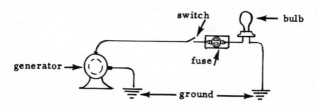

By placing a fuse in the circuit, we can give ourselves a lot of protection from short circuits or overloads, which are almost as dangerous. A fuse is a device that will permit no more than a pre-set amperage to travel through a circuit. Most household fuses are 15-amp jobs; they are plainly marked as to their capacity. If the short or the overload sends more than the pre-set amperage through the circuit, the fuse "blows." That means that the soft wire in the fuse burns out and stops all current from flowing through the circuit.

CONDUCTORS, INSULATORS AND WIRING

Metal, water with salt or other substances dissolved in it, and certain other materials permit electricity to travel along them with relative ease. These materials are called *conductors*. Even among metals, some are better conductors than others. Copper and silver are very good conductors while steel and aluminum are not quite so good. They are good enough, however, to give you quite a jolt if you should happen to touch them when they are charged with electricity, and they are used as conductors for many special purposes. Most electrical wire is made of copper because it does the best job, for its cost, of carrying electricity.

Wood, glass, *dry* cloth, leather, ceramics and rubber are non-conductors, or *insulators*. Rubber is an especially good insulator. That is why linesmen wear rubber gloves and why the insulation on telephone poles is made of special glass or ceramics. Insulated wire is wire covered with rubber, plastic, cloth, or combinations of the three.

You remember reading on page 106 that electricity must have a return to its source, either through the ground or by means of a return wire. If there is no resistance, such as a light bulb, motor, or other appliance between the source of electricity and the return to the source, a short circuit results.

The purpose of wiring is to lead electricity along a good, protected conductor (insulated electrical wire) to where it is needed (the appliance) and back to the source through the ground or a wire. To make the wiring effective, the conducting wire must be heavy enough to take the required amount of current without overheating or burning. The wire must also be insulated all along its surface and at all points where it may come in contact with a ground (return). At the points where wires join to complete a path for electricity, there should be no insulation to block the flow of current. Even dirt can be insulation under these conditions. All connections should be bright and clean; if possible, they should be soldered to keep them that way.

Series and Parallel Wiring. The old-fashioned lights for Christmas trees (they are still sold today) are wired in series. This means that the current flows from one light to another, like this:

The diagram shows eight lights. If the house current is 110 volts, each bulb receives in theory $\frac{1}{8}$ of 110 volts, or about 14 volts; in practice each bulb receives less because of line losses. When one bulb burns out, the whole string goes dark because the pathway for the electricity has been broken. The same thing happens if one bulb is loose in its socket.

The newer lights for Christmas trees are wired in parallel, like this:

The current goes directly to each bulb instead of from one bulb to another. If one light burns out there is still a path for the electricity to flow to the other bulbs. Perhaps this will be clearer in the next diagram:

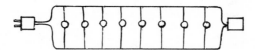

You can see that a burned-out light doesn't cut the flow of electricity to the other bulbs. Each bulb gets the full, theoretical 110 volts. One of the reasons the sockets are larger is to keep you from putting one of the low-voltage series bulbs into the string by mistake.

If you are using dry cells as a source of power, you can produce a stronger current by wiring the dry cells in series. One dry cell, regardless of whether it is a small penlight battery or a large doorbell battery, develops about 1.5 volts. If you put two dry cells in series, they will produce a 3-volt current. Four dry cells will produce a 6-volt current. By connecting enough dry cells in series, you can obtain almost any reasonable voltage you want, in 1.5-volt steps. B Batteries, used in certain portable radio sets, supply 45 volts. They have thirty 1.5-volt cells connected in series. Some radio batteries have combinations of series and parallel hookups to give several different voltages as required by the radio tubes.

If, however, you want only 1.5 volts, but you want the dry cells to last longer, use more dry cells and connect them in parallel.

If you want a 6-volt current with greater amperage than four dry cells can supply, make several sets of four dry cells, wired in series. Wire the whole sets to each other in parallel. You can have fun experimenting with these combinations.

Automobile Storage Batteries. The older type of automobile storage battery develops 6 volts and the new type 12 volts. You can identify them easily—the 6-volt type has three filler caps, and the 12-volt type has six filler caps.

Be careful in handling automobile storage batteries. They have a low voltage but a high amperage.

CHECKING THE FUSES

Even otherwise sensible adults often take chances by overloading electrical circuits, sometimes because they don't know any better, and other times because they just don't want to be bothered. Making a safety check of the fuses is a bit of trouble, but it can save a lot more trouble if it is done properly and if the family will use it as a guide for safe practices.

Don't touch the cartridge fuses! These are the cylindrical jobs that are sprung into place by clips. Only electricians should touch these—never you nor I.

After you open the box, make a diagram and number the fuses in whatever way seems convenient.

Take out fuse No. 1, turning it by the glass part. *Don't touch the metal!* Look behind it for pennies or other things that don't belong there. If you find a coin or other piece of metal, **don't try to take it out.** Pull the main switch before taking it out.

Inspect the fuse, using a brand new fuse for comparison. Check to see if the fuse wire under the plastic window is still unburned. If the number of the fuse is anything other than 15, try to find out why. Remember that most house circuits are designed for 15 amperes, and putting in a 20-amp or larger fuse prevents the fuse from fulfilling its function; it will then permit overloading of the circuit, and consequently will cause fires. It is much better to lighten the load than to put in larger fuses.

No. 1	Living room wall outlets	
	lamp	280 watts
	lamp	100 watts
	television	195 watts
	vacuum cleaner	575 watts
	movie projector	300 watts
	Den overhead lights	150 watts
	wall outlets	
	lamp	100 watts
	desk lamp	40 watts
	Front stoop light	60 watts
		1800 watts

While the fuse is out of the box, see what outlets are dead, and which lights don't light. You can check the outlets with a small lamp that you can carry around, plugging it in as you go. List on your paper the dead outlets and the lights that don't light. If you find any outlet with holes for three prongs instead of two, *leave them alone.* They are designed for heavy appliances and may carry 220 volts instead of the usual 110 or 120.

Add up the wattage of all the lights and appliances on the same circuit as fuse No. 1. To determine the particular circuit controlled by each fuse, turn on all the lights in the house. Loosen the fuses one by one, touching only the glass bulb, *not the metal*. Have a helper walk through the house as you do this and ask him to tell you which set of lights goes out when you loosen each fuse. Note this on your fuse diagram.

Now let's get back to adding up the wattage. A lamp with a 100-watt bulb in it is easy; that's 100 watts, of course. The overhead light in the den might have two 75-watt bulbs in it; that's another 150 watts. Your vacuum cleaner will have a plate on it somewhere that will read "575 watts; 5 amps" or some such reading. In this case, just use the wattage listed. If it doesn't give wattage, but says "7.5 amps," multiply the 7.5 by 110 or 120 (the usual house voltages; find out if yours is different) and you get 825 watts or 900 watts, depending on whether you multiplied by 110 or 120. Most appliances, other than lamps, have a plate on them that lists amps, watts or both.

In the chart, we come up with 1800 watts. Let's assume that your house voltage is 120. Divide the 1800 watts by 120 volts, and the answer is 15 amps, the number allowed by the circuit and the fuse. Although there is no safety margin, this isn't too bad, since it would be most unlikely that the vacuum cleaner and the movie projector would both be running at once. If Mother decides to iron in the living room, however, with a 1000-watt steam iron, look for trouble unless everything else being used at the time on that circuit doesn't exceed 425 watts (assuming the capacity of that circuit to be 1450 watts and leaving a safety margin of 25 watts).

Make a list of the wattage used by the circuit for each fuse. Keep the diagram or list handy. If one circuit begins to blow fuses, you can use the list to help find out if the circuit is overloaded. If it is, explain to the family that some things must be turned off before others are turned on. If it is not overloaded and fuses still blow, try to find out if any particular appliance blows fuses when it is plugged in, or if some switch blows them when it is turned on. Then you can get the appliance checked by a service man, or the switch checked by an electrician.

CHECKING ELECTRICAL WIRES

Fires don't just happen. One frequent cause of home fires is worn or abused wires from appliances to wall outlets. People hardly ever check these wires because they're too busy and because they get interrupted when they start the job. You can save lives and the family fortune by making this simple check. It should be done once a year.

First, make a list of every lamp and appliance in the house, and don't forget the garage and cellar. The list might look like the one below. Be sure to date the page and to check every wire. Here is what to look for:

Broken Plugs. These get broken by being stepped on, by having furniture pushed against them, or by people who pull them out of the outlets by the wire instead of by grasping the plug itself. Check the contacts to see that they are set in solid, and check the wire inside the plug to make sure bare metal portions are not touching, or about to touch.

Worn or Brittle Wires. The thin rubber insulation on most appliances becomes brittle with age and leaves bare the uninsulated wire. This is dangerous and can cause a short circuit and, consequently, a fire. Some pairs of lamp wires are covered with a thin cloth or thread covering; this wears away and exposes the rubber-covered wires underneath.

Be on the lookout especially for worn heavy-duty cords of the type you find on electric irons and toasters. These wear out fairly quickly, exposing a white insulating material. Since these appliances draw heavy current, they are particularly open to short circuits.

September 1, 196 –
SAFETY CHECK OF WIRING

Appliance	Location	Condition of Wire	Condition of Plug	Condition of Switch
Lamp, floor	Den	Dry, cracked	OK	Gets hot
Electric clock	Den	Good	Prongs loose	—
Lamp, desk	Den	Thread worn	Good	OK
Refrigerator	Kitchen	Good	Good	—
Toaster	Kitchen	Insulation worn	Good	—
Electric clock	Kitchen	Good	Smashed	—
(etc.)				

Extension Cords. Often when the cord that comes with an appliance doesn't reach to the wall outlet, families make them reach by using an extension cord. Watch out for extension cords that are more than a few feet long; using a long, light-duty extension cord is just begging for trouble. Extension cords shouldn't run under rugs or other places where they might become worn. Nor should they be in places where people are likely to trip over them. When someone trips on an extension cord, he may not only hurt himself, but may also pull the cord from the wall and tip over and break appliances.

It's not wise to use a light-duty extension cord to make a heavy-duty appliance reach the wall. If the appliance has a heavy rubber cord or an asbestos-covered cord attached to it, it just isn't safe to let a thin lamp cord carry the current the rest of the way to the wall.

Switches. Switches on appliances often go bad and are not attended to. Look for switches that get hot, that don't work every time, that feel loose, or that require too hard an effort to flick on or off.

REMOVING A BROKEN LIGHT BULB

Once in a great while, when you are removing a burned-out electric light bulb, the glass will separate from the metal. It is possible to get the metal out, though. The following procedures can come in handy if a bulb is broken, too.

First, be doubly sure the current is off. If you have a large cork, jam it right over the broken glass and turn the cork.

If the glass has merely separated from the metal part of the bulb, another way to get the metal out is to keep twisting until the parts separate and the glass comes out. If the glass is broken, pick the pieces away from the metal with a pair of pliers. Then with a small screw driver, force the blade between the brass end of the bulb and the brass inside the socket. When, by this method, you have gotten enough room to grip the brass bottom of the bulb with long-nosed pliers, do so, and use the pliers to turn the brass counterclockwise. When you get it loose enough, finish the job with *gloved* fingers; use the gloves so you won't cut yourself on any remaining pieces of glass.

REPLACING BROKEN PLUGS THE EASY WAY

Let's suppose your check of the wiring turns up a smashed plug hidden behind the living room sofa. It's the plug for a lamp that doesn't carry too much current, and the wire from the lamp to the plug is in good shape. Only the plug needs to be replaced and a light-duty one will work.

Your local hardware store has the answer to this one, and you can fix it in less than three minutes. It is a patented plug (called a "pin-on plug cap") with a removable core, and it looks like this:

Trim your wire off even; do *not* strip any insulation. Remove the core of the plug from the outer case. Run the wire through the outer case of the plug. Be sure the "wings" on the inner core are in the "out" position. Run the two strands of the wire into the holes in the core as far as they will go. Squeeze the "wings" together. Slip the core back into the outer case. The job is done, and the "wings" are the prongs that go into the wall socket.

Perhaps the hardware store doesn't have the type of plug that is so very easy to attach, or perhaps you want something a bit stronger to resist the shock when the sofa is jammed against the wall again. Or perhaps there is one of the older types of plugs in your junk box. You had better know how to replace this kind also.

Cut the end of the cord clean, as close to the plug as you can. Push the end of the cord through the hole in the plug from the rear, like this:

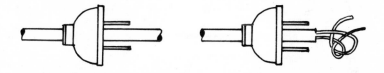

Strip off several inches of the braid that holds the two wires together, being very careful to avoid damaging the rubber insulation beneath the braid. If the cord has two rubber-covered wires pressed together, separate them carefully for a couple of inches.

Now tie an electrician's knot. Then pull the plug against the cord so the knot fits tightly in the space provided for it. This little trick, rarely done by most home fix-it experts, will protect the wire and the plug from those people who insist on pulling out plugs by the wires instead of by the plug itself.

Next, cut off the ends of the wires at a length that will permit them to make a full turn under the screws in the plug. Then, very carefully, strip off the insulation from the ends, being sure you don't injure the wire strands. Twist the strands into a solid rope. Scrape them with a knife until the copper is bright. Bend the brightened ends under the screw heads in a clockwise direction, so that when you tighten the screw the friction between screw and wire will tighten the wire around the threaded portion of the screw. If you are to wind the wires counter-clockwise, tightening the screw would have the effect of loosening the coil.

Check to be sure that your two wires are not touching at any place where there is no insulation. Replace the fiber cap if there is one; if not, perhaps a piece of friction tape will make a satisfactory cover.

Try the lamp, or appliance. No fuses blown? You did it!

INSTALLING A CORD SWITCH

The cord switch is one of the handiest gadgets to appear since the invention of the bottle opener. It's surprising, too, how many adult home handy men never heard of these useful little devices.

The switch looks like this:

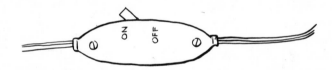

If you have ever installed or repaired a faulty plug (see page 114), you will find installing the cord switch extremely easy. Take off the cover and look at the switch, and you'll see how to do it. Just remember to install it neatly so the loose wire ends don't touch each other in places where they're not supposed to.

You can install it in the cord to almost any electrical appliance that doesn't use heavy-duty wire, and it is especially useful for extension cords and Christmas tree lights. Most circuits for Christmas trees are set up so that you have to pull the plug out of the outlet to turn out the lights, and put it back in to turn them on. This is rough on plugs and also on chubby parents if the outlet is along the baseboard of the wall, as it usually is. Install the switch at some convenient place along the extension cord between the plug and the tree. Then you can light the tree with just a flip of the thumb.

You will undoubtedly think of other uses for the cord switch.

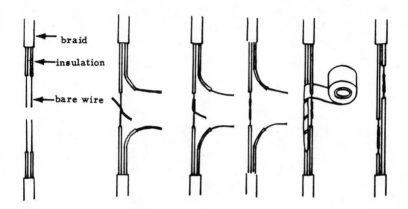

SPLICING LAMP CORD

Now that you have replaced a plug, the time has come to try your hand at splicing lamp cord. This is a job that you can do, but it requires care and neatness. Try it first on a piece of cord that isn't connected to anything, just for practice.

Remove the braid and inner insulation from two ends of lamp cord, just as you did to connect the plug. Follow the first five steps as illustrated. Using friction tape, tape both wires so that no metal from one spliced side touches metal from the other; this would cause a short circuit.

Then wrap the whole thing with friction tape. It looks sort of bulky, doesn't it?

Try it again, this time making the cuts at alternate places on the wires so you end up with something that looks like the sixth step. This will result in a longer but thinner taped area. There is less chance also of metal touching metal this way since the insulation will help prevent shorts.

REWIRING A LAMP

Now that you can splice lamp cord and replace a plug, it is time to replace one of those dangerous wires you found when you checked wires.

Be sure the lamp is disconnected, of course. Take apart carefully and slowly the upper works of the lamp. Make a sketch of what you take apart so you can get it together again the same way. When you get the brass cylinder widget off the lamp stand, you'll see a placed marked "Press." When you press, you can pull off the top of the widget. See the illustration.

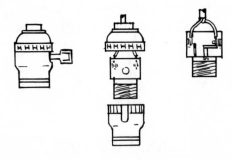

Don't unfasten the wires yet. If you pull the wire through, you might have a hard time getting the new wire in. Tie a knot between the old wire and the new. Then pull the old wire gently but firmly, thus using the old wire to pull the new wire through. When you get enough of the new wire up into the head of the lamp, disconnect it from the old wire. Then scrape the insulation from the new wire and fasten it down much as you did when you replaced the plug (see page 116).

When you get the lamp top put together again, be sure you don't let the cord running from the base stretch out more than about 6 feet. Longer cords are dangerous.

TAKING CARE OF VARIOUS ELECTRICAL APPLIANCES

You must realize to begin with that modern appliances are baffling, even to home "do-it-yourself" experts of many years' experience. Many are so complicated in design that repairs really require factory-trained men using special tools. Sometimes it seems that the manufacturers do this on purpose to keep "do-it-yourselfers" from ruining their own appliances. My own electric razor offers an example of the problems you face when you try to do your own repairs. Every six months or so, the brushes need cleaning or replacing, but I have never been able to figure out how to take the two plastic halves apart to reach the brushes, and no service man will tell me how. They just smile and say, "We have the factory equipment to do the job." What's worse, even if I could get the halves apart myself I probably couldn't buy brushes of the right size and type. When a cycling device on a washing machine, for example, goes bad, you might as well give up right away and call the repair man. You probably need a new cycling device, which is so expensive in itself that you might as well have the repair man install it too.

If you do go ahead and work on a "sick" appliance, don't try to do repairs much more extensive than those described in the accompanying instruction booklet. Don't *force* things apart. If a part doesn't unscrew easily, it's probably not meant to come apart except at the factory or an authorized repair shop.

Air Conditioners. There isn't much you can do yourself for your air conditioner, except to lubricate it according to the accompanying instruction booklet. Of course, you should keep the grills and louvers clean and check the set screws for tightness. If anything serious goes wrong, though, call the repair man.

Electric Irons. You need special tools to take most modern irons apart and replace a burned-out heating element. If you succeed in getting the iron apart without special tools, however, go to a good electric supply store for a new heating element. Take the old one with you so you'll get the same kind. Be sure also to tell the salesman the make, size and model number of the iron.

Electric Toasters. You can forestall the need for repairs by keeping the crumbs cleaned out. Replacing the heating element, if you should have to do it, is fairly easy on most brands. Take the toaster apart carefully so you will remember how the parts fit together. Put in the new heating element and put the toaster together again. Don't try to repair the timing mechanism if anything goes wrong with it; amateurs are rarely successful with these.

Electric Dishwashers. Mechanical trouble with dishwashers usually stems from the cycling device—and this is for experts. If, however, the trouble consists of water spilling onto the floor, check for obstructions around the breather pipe. Make sure also that if the dishwasher drains into a disposal sink, the disposal is empty, or if it drains into an ordinary sink, be sure that the sink itself drains properly (see page 94).

TAKING CARE OF A TELEVISION SET

Most of us are not electronic wizards, but you don't have to be to prevent some of the calls to the TV service men; in most cities every call you can prevent saves at least five dollars and often more than that.

There are many makes and models of TV sets. Basically they are very much alike, but there are enough differences to cause all kinds of difficulties if I were to try to give you a short course in TV maintenance and repair. All I can do is to offer some general hints. The book that came with the set, particularly if it offers a wiring diagram, will be a great help to you. The back panel of many sets is also full of information; read it carefully and pay attention to what you read.

The first thing to remember, if you start to work on a TV set, is *never, never* to stick your fingers into a set that is connected to a power source. Pull the plug out! Secondly, a dangerous charge of static electricity may be present at two points in your set, *even with the power off.* Believe me, there can be a painful jolt of static electricity at the base of the high-voltage rectifier tube or on the back surface of a metal picture tube. I strongly recommend that before you go into the set's innards, you have a TV service man show you how to neutralize these two static charges. The book that comes with the set may tell you how to do this, but that's not enough. Have the TV service man show you even if you think you understand the diagram perfectly.

Let's assume now that you have learned how to neutralize the static electricity in the set and you are about to inspect it because it hasn't been working well. First, check the antenna to see that it has no broken wires, that it is screwed up tight to the set, and that the terminals are clean and bright. Then try the wall outlet with an appliance other than the TV set, such as a lamp; perhaps the trouble lies with the power source. Next, check the wire from the set to the wall for breaks in the insulation or the copper, and check the plug too.

If all these things seem to be in order, read all the instructions on the back of the set, and then remove the back, but not far enough to disconnect the interlock. Practically every set has an interlock that is designed to disconnect the power automatically when you take off the back cover. The power is on, so *keep your fingers out of the set*. Look at the tubes carefully. Is one glowing purple? Is one cold entirely? Is one flashing? If so, these tubes are suspect; note where they are.

Take the back of the set off all the way now, turn off the set, and pull out the plug. When the set cools, remove the suspect tubes.

To remove tubes, rock them very gently from side to side, at the same time pulling them upward. Don't get rough; you can do a lot of damage to the set and your fingers if you do. Some tubes have metal shields; if so, you have to remove the shield either first or together with the tube, depending on how tight the shield fits. Do *not* replace the tube without the shield.

If you take out many tubes, mark them on a homemade diagram so you can replace them in the same spot. Many tubes won't fit in the wrong place, but some will. Each tube has a number; mark your diagram to indicate where the tube with that number goes. There may be a diagram inside the set or in the instruction book which can save you this trouble, but be sure you can read the diagram before you trust it.

Take the suspect tubes to the nearest tube tester, which you may find at a large drug store, a hardware store, or any other place that sells TV tubes. Read the directions on the tester, and give the tubes the recommended tests. Remember that a tube cannot be "pretty good." It either tests out completely or needs to be replaced. Using a weak or otherwise defective tube may put a strain on other tubes, and you will lose money in the long run instead of saving it.

When you replace the tubes after testing, be sure that you put everything back the way it was, and that you haven't knocked any wires adrift or forgotten to replace a tube or two. If the suspect tubes pass the test, or if they fail but the replacement tubes still do not clear up the trouble, you will have to go a little deeper. Perhaps it's time to test *all* the tubes. This is quite a job, but it should be done about once a year in any event. If the set still doesn't work properly after you have tested all the tubes and replaced those that didn't pass the test, then there is nothing to do but call the service man. If he fixes the set by replacing something other than a tube, you still belong at the head of the class.

One thing that most TV owners neglect to do is to clean the outside of the picture tube and both sides of the glass shield in front of it. Cleaning these surfaces of several years' worth of dust and grime can make all the difference in the world in the picture. Many sets are built so you can take the glass off the front by snapping off the dials and loosening a few screws or nuts. On some sets, you must remove the chassis from its case to reach the inside of the glass. When you clean, have the set turned off and cool, and treat the picture tube with care. If it is covered with sticky grease and film, use a window-cleaning preparation or put some vinegar in the water. Don't slop the water around; water and electrical appliances don't mix well at all.

MAKING A CRAZY LIGHT BOX

If there is a child between the ages of four and eight in your family, you can make him the most spectacular toy he ever owned, and one that he will remember all his life. It will cost you a few cents, a lot of ingenuity and a fair amount of work.

The materials required are simple:

A wooden box about 20 inches by 14 inches by 10 inches. It can be larger or smaller and you can either find it or make it.

Many small knife switches, doorbell buttons, flashlight batteries, electric buzzers, electric bells, and other gadgets that interrupt electric current, that light up, and that make a noise.

Yards and yards of light bell wire or the kind of wire used in electric train sets.

Some flashlight batteries, or radio B or C batteries.

Put the batteries in the box and attach the lighting gadgets to the

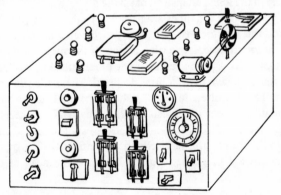

top of the box. Put the switches and buttons on the front. The buzzers and bells can go on a side of the box.

Now try your hand at some real crazy wiring. You can put your switches in series (see page 108) so that it takes a certain combination of switches to ring a particular bell or to light a particular light. Other switches may actuate both a light and a buzzer or several lights. The less rhyme or reason to how it is wired, the more fun it will be.

There are a few cautions to remember as you build this gadget panel:

Do *not* hook it up to house current, not even with a transformer. Things can go wrong and young children can get a shock easily.

Don't wire in any short circuits.

Watch for sharp edges, especially raw-edged sheet metal. Conceal them in the panel or pad them with tape.

Make a wiring diagram as you go. You might find it very useful for reconstruction if the child, as usually happens, decides to do some rewiring on his own.

The more combinations of things you can do with the box, the better it will be as a toy. And don't you believe it if someone tells you it's too complicated for little Billy. Give him a few hours with it and he'll show you combinations you forgot you had put into the box.

TAKING CARE OF A RADIO

If the radio goes completely dead, first check your wall outlet with a lamp, or try the set in another outlet. If the outlet is all right, feel the entire length of the cord for breaks. If the cord seems to be in good order, carefully take off the back of the set. Don't disturb the antenna inside the set if there is one there. Look for broken wires and connections. If there are none, then check the tubes at a tube tester.

The circuits of the smaller sets are often laid out in series (see page 108), so you have to check all the tubes. Believe it or not, if the dial lamp persists in burning out, it may be because of a faulty tube.

On 3-way (combination portable and "plug-in" radios) and battery sets, the batteries are always suspect, especially if the radio operates for a short period and dies out.

If the volume varies without apparent reason, try rotating the appliance plug 180 degrees in the wall outlet. This often gets rid of the antenna effect of the house wiring.

If none of these approaches work, take the set to the repair man.

Safety in the Home

We have mentioned safety and safe practices throughout this book, but safety is just a word until we begin to think about it seriously. When people get hurt or killed unnecessarily, it is tragic. If it happens because of something we might have foreseen and prevented, the tragedy is compounded.

One of our most famous railroads does not believe in the slogan "Safety First!" Rather, they have adopted the slogan, "Safety Always!"

Often out of sheer force of habit we accept certain activities and conditions that can lead, sooner or later, to someone's getting hurt (or worse), or to fire or other property damage.

Let's look around the house for some of these trouble-breeders.

STORING INFLAMMABLE LIQUIDS

Chances are that your household is one of the many that commit common breaches of safety rules. Your parents might be annoyed with you for mentioning it unless you do it in a *very* nice way.

Look around the house for glass containers of gasoline, kerosene, lighter fluid, even turpentine—any of the liquids used for cleaning or thinning paint, that are explosive or that catch on fire quickly.

Glass is not the proper container. Mother drops it, the kitten rubs against it and it drops off the shelf, or you trip over it, and there it is on the floor, building up dangerous vapors that can be touched off by turning on a faulty light switch, the pilot light of a stove, or a struck match. And when one of these fluids is vaporized, its explosive force is just like the mixture in an automobile cylinder, only worse.

If you have any influence with the people who make the decisions in your home, use it to see that these items are kept in shatterproof containers only. Even with the proper containers it is best to keep these materials out of the house entirely except when they are being used. Many families use an outdoor paint locker to store these dangerous liquids. You might make one out of a good wooden packing box. Fit a door and lock to it, and weatherproof it with batting or in some other manner.

PREVENTING SPONTANEOUS COMBUSTION

Not all home fires start in the electrical system or from gas leaks or spilled volatile liquids. Many begin from something called spontaneous combustion. Spontaneous combustion occurs when oily rags, paper or other combustible material like straw or excelsior is permitted to lie around in a confined space. Plain moisture under certain conditions can produce on the fibers of these materials a chemical reaction that releases heat. In a confined space, the temperature builds up until it reaches the combustion point of the materials or of something surrounding them—and listen to those fire sirens!

I helped put out one fire that began in the hip pocket of a man's overalls, only he wasn't wearing them at the time. Mr. King had been staining the wood trim of his new cabin with a rag dipped in a mixture of gasoline and tar. Before he went back to the city on Sunday afternoon, he stuck the rag in the hip pocket of his overalls and hung them on a peg in the cabin in a tightly closed closet. A passing neighbor smelled smoke the next morning—it happened that fast.

Search the house for rags that have been in paint or grease or furniture polish. Wash them or throw them away. If Mother won't let you do either of these things to her prized furniture polish rag, try to get her to spread it out unfolded where it can get plenty of air.

PREVENTING FIRES CAUSED BY FURNACES AND STOVES

Most furnaces and stoves have been installed by people who knew what they were doing, but occasionally they are placed too close to combustible materials, such as wood or wallboard. Sometimes the wood or wallboard has been installed after the furnace. When the furnace or stove is hot, feel all the wood or other combustible surfaces nearby. If the surface feels uncomfortably hot, or if you see charred places, mention it to your parents.

Some home fires are caused by plain carelessness, like leaving a pasteboard box on top of a cold furnace "just for an hour or two until I find a place to put it," and the hour or two drags out for several days until the furnace turns on. Other home fires are caused by papers being blown onto a lighted gas burner on a stove. The women, wanting to dry something in a hurry, may hang things over a stove or furnace, and leave them there until they catch on fire.

Just keep an eye open for these hazards. You only have to prevent one fire in your lifetime to make it worth while.

CHECKING LADDERS

Are there any ladders around the house? Look them over. You might save someone a nasty fall.

If you have a folding ladder, set it up in extended position and test it for wobbling. If it wobbles, locate the source. Perhaps tightening a screw or two is the answer. Or you might have to brace it with cross strips of light wood, using screws, *not* nails. Of course, if it wobbles too much and is put together with nails, screws in place of nails all around might save it from the junkpile. But don't just let it wobble; wobbling ladders either move, collapse, or both.

If the ladder passes the wobble test, check it over completely for cracks that weaken the structure. Search especially for cracked steps that might give way when someone is using the ladder.

Most folding ladders have a folding shelf for buckets. Be sure that this shelf is extended out when the ladder is in use (it adds stability) but first check to be sure the shelf won't give way under a load. See that the wood isn't brittle, that the nails are tight, and that there are no cracks.

The long ladders that lean against a house or roof are even more treacherous. The rungs look perfectly safe when they might be dry-rotted through. Check each rung carefully. If it seems suspicious, try jabbing the suspicious spots with an ice pick. You will be able to tell if the wood is rotten if the pick goes into it too easily.

Be sure the ladders are stored indoors in a dry place. There is less chance of damage to the wood this way.

And when you use one of these non-folding types, do what telephone linemen do. Be sure that the bottom of the ladder is one quarter its length away from the wall. If your ladder is 16 feet long the bottom should be 4 feet away from the wall it is leaning against.

CHECKING RAILINGS

Railings are designed for protection against falls. Some are meant to hold on to while using the stairs, others are meant to prevent people from falling from high places.

Since people lean on railings, a railing that is not properly fastened or one that has rotted or rusted to the point of weakness is more dangerous than no railing at all.

Look over all the railings in the house. Try shaking them. It won't be hard to tell if they are too loose and why they are loose. Rap on wooden railings with a stick. You'll know by the sound if the wood is solid or rotted. Iron railings that have been permitted to rust need more examination; be sure they haven't rusted through or nearly through. Inspect the joints carefully; often that is where the trouble lies.

Repair or replacement of unsafe railings depends on many things, such as the extent, difficulty, expense and necessity of the repair. If your family decides to let you do the repair, you'll find that rusty iron railings are fun to take care of. Get all the rust off with a good rust-preventive coat before you paint them and then use a good metal paint in an attractive color.

KEEPING THE WIND FROM SLAMMING DOORS

In many homes there is one particular door that the wind plays tricks with, slamming it with a violence that doesn't match the wind velocity outside. Occasionally one of these doors will slam at just the right instant to catch an unwary finger in the jamb. That is a painful experience.

If your house has one of these unpredictable doors, don't wait until somebody gets a mashed finger.

Buy a screen-door hook and screw-eye set; mount the eye on the door and the hook on the molding at the bottom of the wall. Then keep the door closed with the hook.

INDEX

Air conditioners, 119
Alternating current, 105
Amps, 105
Appliances,
  electrical, 118-122,123
  instruction notebook for, 75
Applying paint, 9-10
Attic, flooring an, 47-48
Automobile. See Car.

Backsaw, 31
Basement, painting in the, 14
Battery of car, 59-60, 110
Bird feeder, making a, 52-53
Block plane, 33, 35
Bolts, nuts and, 26-27
Bookshelves, making, 45-46
Built-in cabinets, adjusting
  doors of, 77-78

Cabinets, putting wheels on, 51
Cabinets, built-in, adjusting
  doors of, 77-78
Candlesticks, Christmas,
  making, 40-41
Car, care of, 56-66
Car, tightening screws of, 60
Carrier for firewood,
  making a, 46-47
Caulking, 81-82
Compass, 26
Compass saw, 31-32
Concrete floors, painting, 15
Conductors, 108
Coping saw, 32
Cord switch,
  installing a, 116-117
Creative projects, easy, 40-55
Current, alternating, 105
  direct, 106
Cutting grass, 68-70
Cycles, electrical, 105-106

Designs with masking tape, 16
Direct current, 106
Dishwashers, 119-120
Doors, unsticking, 78-79
  keeping wind from slam-
  ming, 127
Drains, unplugging, 94-95

Electrical appliances,
  118-122, 123
  instruction notebook for, 75
Electrical terms, basic, 105-106
Electrical theory,
  basic, 106-107
Electrical toy, 122-123
Electrical wires, 112-114
Electric fans, 76-77
Electricity, household, 104-123
Extension cords, 113-114

Fans, electric, 76-77
Faucets, leaky, 97-98
Fires from furnaces and stoves,
  preventing, 125-126
Firewood, making a
  carrier for, 46-47
Folding rule, 25
Freeze-prevention of liquids, 91
Fuel, saving, 100-101
Furnace, schedule
  for care of, 76

Furnaces and stoves, preventing fires from, 125-126
Fuses, 110-112

Garage guide, 65-66
Garbage disposals,
  clogged, 98-99
Garden, care of, 72-74
Garden tools, 72-74
Gas leaks, 99-100
Guide for putting car
  in garage, 65-66
Gutters and leaders, 90

Hack saw, 32
Hammers, 28-29
Hand saws, 29-31
Hand tools, 19-20
Heating, care of the, 99-103
Home maintenance,
  tricks for easier, 75-93
House plants, care of, 68

Inflammable liquids,
  storing, 124-125
Insulators, 108
Interior walls and ceiling,
  painting, 17-18
Irons, electric, 119

Jack, bumper, 63, 64
Jack plane, 33, 34

Kerf, 30
Keyhole saw. See Compass
  saw.
Kilowatt-hour, 105
Kilowatts, 105

Ladders, checking, 126
Lamp cord, splicing, 117
Lamp, rewiring a, 118
Lamp, table, making a, 48-50
Lawn, garden and house
  plants, care of, 67-74
Leaders, 90
Leaks, gas, 99-100
Leaky faucets, 97-98
Light bulb, broken,
  removing a, 114
Lights of car, 59-60
Liquids, freeze-
  prevention of, 91
Loose-leaf binder,
  making a, 44-45
Lumber, 37-38
Luminous paint, tricks with, 16
Lug wrench, marking a, 62

Main shut-off valve, 93
Main switch, 104
Maintenance record
  for car, 56-57
Masking tape, designs with, 16
Measuring tools, 25-26
Mounting things
  in plaster, 91-92

Nail, driving a, 36-37
Nails, language of, 35-36
Nuts and bolts, 26-27

Oil, lights and battery
  of car, 58-60

Paintbrushes, 10-12
Painting, 7-18
Parallel wiring, 108-110

Pegboard, hanging a, 53-55
Pipes, frozen, thawing, 96
Planes, 32-35
Plaques, making, 42-44
Plaster, mounting
  things in, 91-92
Pliers, 27-28
Plugs, broken, 113
  replacing, 114-116
Plumbing and heating,
  care of the, 93-103
Porch, screening a, 89-90
Porch steps, painting, 13
Preparations for painting, 7-9

Radiators, leaky and
  noisy, fixing, 102-103
Radio, taking care of, 123
Railings, checking, 127
  outside metal,
  painting, 12-13
Reel for storing lines,
  making a, 41-42
Rotary mower, 68-70
Rule, folding, 25

Safety, home, 124-127
Saws, 29-32
Screens and screen doors, 82-89
Screw drivers, 21-22
Screw head, ruined, 23-24
Screws of car, keeping tight, 60
Screws, wood, 22-23
Series and parallel
  wiring, 108-110
Short circuit, 107
Shut-off valve, main, 93
Smoothing plane, 33, 34
"Snake," using the, 95
Spontaneous combustion, 125
Sprays and sprayers,
  garden, 74
Squares for measuring, 25
Steps, warped, 79-80
Storing lines, making a
  reel for, 41-42
Switch cord,
  installing a, 116-117
Switch, main, 104

Television set, care of, 120-122
Tire, changing a, 62-65
Tire pressures, 57-58
Toasters, electric, 119
Toilet tanks, dripping, 96-97
Tools, 19-39
Toy, electrical,
  making an, 122-123

Valve, main shut-off, 93
Volts, 105, 106

Warped steps, repairing, 79-80
Washing car, 60-62
Wastebasket, making a, 55
Watts, 105
Watering the lawn, 67-68
Windows, checking
  screens of, 82-83
  making screens for, 84-89
  unsticking, 80-81
Wires, electrical, 112-114
Wiring, 108-110
Wood screws, 22-23
Wrenches, 26-27